The Real Number System
in an Algebraic Setting

A Series of Undergraduate Books in Mathematics
R. A. Rosenbaum, EDITOR

Introduction to Matrices and Linear Transformations
Daniel T. Finkbeiner, II

Introduction to Probability and Statistics
Henry L. Alder and Edward B. Roessler

Golden Gate Books

A Concrete Approach to Abstract Algebra
W. S. Sawyer

A Modern View of Geometry
Leonard M. Blumenthal

Sets, Logic, and Axiomatic Theories
Robert R. Stoll

The Solution of Equations in Integers
A. O. Gelfond

An Elementary Introduction to the Theory of Probability
B. V. Gnedenko and A. Ya. Khinchin

The Real Number System in an Algebraic Setting
J. B. Roberts

The Real

Number System

in an

Algebraic Setting

by **J. B. ROBERTS**

REED COLLEGE

W. H. Freeman and Company

SAN FRANCISCO AND LONDON

Preface

THIS course of study is intended to acquaint the student with the basic facts of a mathematical system of great importance. The course, while being quite detailed and technical, is of great cultural value to nonscience students. It seems that one cannot have any real understanding of what mathematics is about, what its methods are, and what is meant by mathematical creativity without having detailed experience in some technical aspect of mathematics.

Because of its beauty and intrinsic interest, as well as its complexity, the real number system is an excellent vehicle for conveying to the beginner the power and precision of a mathematical system. A wealth of methods, ideas, and techniques is necessarily placed in the forefront.

In this course I have tried to use those methods which will be of greatest importance in future work. Many important ideas from algebra are introduced early. At the same time I have tried to presuppose nothing more than that the student be familiar with the basic properties of the natural numbers and that he be willing to think hard about the subject. Chapter II is devoted to a discussion of the mathematics assumed. The text itself is not complete. Many gaps are left to be filled by completing the exercises; thus many of the exercises must be regarded as part of the text. These are marked with an asterisk. The student should certainly work all of these and in general should work every exercise.

No proofs are given in the first section of Chapter VI. In this section are presented all definitions and theorems needed to carry out the development of the set of all real numbers from the set of nonnegative real numbers. It is suggested that the student complete this task on his own or for an outside examination. Treated in this way, much of the course becomes integrated in the student's mind. More important, he gains confidence in his ability to carry out a complicated bit of reasoning.

It is almost inevitable that sometime during the course there will be questions about infinite sets and infinite cardinal numbers. To satisfy the student's needs, two appendixes introduce these notions. These appendixes are not necessary to the main development and may be omitted from it. Also included as an appendix is a short introduction to the complex numbers.

This book is the outgrowth of a set of notes that have undergone almost continuous transformation since they were first written in 1956–1957. During each of the past five years I have used them in my classes, and during the past four years several of my colleagues at Reed College have used them. I do not delude myself into thinking that the material cannot be further improved and would welcome any suggestions.

July 1961   J. B. Roberts

Contents

Cardinal Numbers

Interlude, In Which the Way is Prepared

The Nonnegative Real Numbers

CHAPTER **VI**

The Real Numbers

APPENDIX A.

Cardinal Numbers (continued)

I   Introduction

I.1. Collections and Cartesian Products

When we speak of a *collection* in mathematics we intend roughly the same meaning as when the word is used in everyday language. Thus, if we are considering the first five natural numbers denoted by 1, 2, 3, 4, 5, we speak of the collection $\{1, 2, 3, 4, 5\}$; the names of the individual elements (or members) of the collection are enclosed in brackets.

The collection $\{\Delta, *, \square\}$ has three elements whose names are Δ, $*$, and $\square$. There are many other collections such as:

(1) The collection Z of all natural numbers: $\{1, 2, 3, \cdots\}$. (Here the three dots indicate that the string of numbers in the collection continues in a similar way indefinitely.)

(2) The collection of all even natural numbers: $\{2, 4, 6, \cdots\}$.

(3) The collection of all natural numbers less than or equal to 20: $\{1, 2, 3, \cdots, 20\}$. (Here the three dots indicate that the string of numbers in the collection continues in a similar way until 20 is reached, at which place the string stops.)

(4) The collection of all living people. (We do not try to use the bracket notation in a case such as this.)

(5) The collection of Reed College freshman girls.

(6) The collection of all living centaurs. (This collection has no members and is therefore referred to as the *empty set*. It may seem strange to speak of such a set, but we shall see later that it is a very useful concept. We consider the set of all living centaurs to be the same as the set of all men over 20 feet tall; that is, there is only one empty set. The empty set is denoted by $\varnothing$.)

1

Note that a collection cannot contain a given element more than once.

Several words are used synonymously with the word "collection." In this text we shall use "set" and "class." Thus, the collection $\{1, 2\}$ will often be called the set $\{1, 2\}$ or the class $\{1, 2\}$.

If each element of one set A is an element of a second set B, then we call the set A a *subset* of the set B. In particular, both B and $\emptyset$ are subsets of B. The subsets of the set $\{a, b, c\}$ are $\emptyset$, $\{a\}$ $\{b\}$, $\{c\}$, $\{a, b\}$, $\{a, c\}$, $\{b, c\}$, and $\{a, b, c\}$.

A *proper subset* of a set is any subset other than the empty set and the set itself. Thus, the proper subsets of $\{a, b, c\}$ are all those subsets listed above except the first and the last.

Quite often the collections we wish to consider have as elements not single members or objects, as in the above examples, but sets of objects. For instance, the collection

$$\{\{1, 2\}, \{2, 3\}, \{1, 3\}, \{2, 4\}\}$$

has as elements the sets $\{1, 2\}$, $\{2, 3\}$, $\{1, 3\}$, and $\{2, 4\}$. Thus, this is a set of sets (or a collection of sets).

When we write

$$\{a, b, c\}$$

we are dealing with a collection containing as elements the objects denoted by a, b, and c. These objects are not ordered in any special way—of course we must write their names in some order, but the order is not to be regarded as being of any significance. In this light, all of the expressions

$$\{a, b, c\}, \{b, c, a\}, \{b, a, c\}$$

are names for the same collection and we write

$$\{a, b, c\} = \{b, c, a\} = \{b, a, c\}.$$

In general, two sets are equal if and only if they have exactly the same elements.

Sometimes we do wish to take order into account, and we shall often speak of ordered pairs, ordered triples, and so on. The set $\{a, b\}$ is the same as the set $\{b, a\}$, as observed above. However, the elements in this set can be arranged in the two orders as exhibited. If we wish to consider this set in a specific order, then we shall use parentheses around the elements of the set rather than brackets. Thus, we write

$$(a, b)$$

for the set $\{a, b\}$ when a is regarded as the "first" and b the "second" element. Similarly, we shall write

$$(b, a)$$

for the set $\{a, b\}$ when b is regarded as the first and a the second element. We shall also speak of ordered pairs of the form (a, a), even though there is no set $\{a, a\}$ (since this violates the condition that a set have no element repeated).

Because of these conventions we have

$$\{a, b\} = \{b, a\},$$

while

$$(a, b) \neq (b, a),$$

unless $a = b$. We can speak of ordered triples, ordered quadruples, and so on in a similar way.

Making use of the notion of ordered pair we may introduce the concept of the *Cartesian product* of two sets. We shall use capital Roman letters for sets. Thus, we might use the letter A for the set $\{a, b, c\}$ and the letter B for the set $\{\Delta, *\}$.

If A and B are sets, then the Cartesian product of A and B, written A $\times$ B, is defined to be the collection of all ordered pairs of the form (a, b), where a is an element of A and b is an element of B. For example, if

$$A = \{a, b, c\}$$

and

$$B = \{\Delta, *\},$$

then

$$A \times B = \{(a, \Delta), (a, *), (b, \Delta), (b, *), (c, \Delta), (c, *)\}.$$

Is B $\times$ A the same as A $\times$ B? Computing B $\times$ A gives

$$B \times A = \{(\Delta, a), (\Delta, b), (\Delta, c), (*, a), (*, b), (*, c)\}.$$

Direct inspection shows

$$A \times B \neq B \times A.$$

Another example of a Cartesian product is as follows. Let A be the collection of all natural numbers and B be the collection of all odd natural numbers. Then

$$A = \{1, 2, 3, \cdots\};$$
$$B = \{1, 3, 5, \cdots\};$$
$$A \times B = \{(1, 1), (1, 3), (1, 5), \cdots$$
$$(2, 1), (2, 3), (2, 5), \cdots$$
$$(3, 1), (3, 3), (3, 5), \cdots$$
$$\cdots\cdots\cdots\cdots\cdots\cdots\cdots\}.$$

● **EXERCISES**

1. Under what conditions will $A \times B = B \times A$?

2. Let $A = \{a, b, c\}$, $B = \{\Delta, *\}$, $C = \{1\}$. Compute $(A \times B) \times C$ and $A \times (B \times C)$. Are they the same?

3. Let A be the set of all real numbers. Exhibit a correspondence between the elements of $A \times A$ and the points on a plane.

4. Show that the points on the surface of a torus (a doughnut-shaped region of space) can be made to correspond to the elements of a Cartesian product $A \times B$, where A is the set of points on the circumference of one circle and B is the set of points on the circumference of a second circle.

I.2. Mappings

It is often convenient for illustrative purposes to think of a collection as several dots inside an oval. For instance, the collection $\{1, 2, 3, 4, 5\}$ might be illustrated as follows.

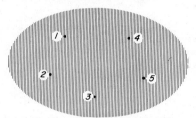

Often in mathematics we wish to correspond to each element of one collection, say A, a unique element of a second collection, say B. Pictorially, we might have the following.

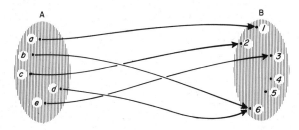

Note that each element of A is "tied to" an element of B. Further, each element of A is tied to only one element of B. We could denote this correspondence by a single letter, say f. Then f makes correspond to a the number 1, to b the number 6, to c the number 2, and so on. We call f a *mapping* of A into B. Further, we say the *image* of a under the mapping f is 1, the *image* of b under the mapping f is 6, and so on. We write

$$f(a) = 1,$$
$$f(b) = 6,$$

and so on.

We now give a tentative definition of mapping. A *mapping* of a set A into a set B is a rule which associates to each element of A a unique element of B.

With this definition in mind we can think of a mapping in two ways. First, we can think of it dynamically as a process which takes each element of A into an element of B. This is the thought process corresponding to the following picture. Second, we can

think of it as a collection of ordered pairs of elements, the first of which is taken from A and the second of which is taken from B, such that each element of A is the first element of exactly one ordered pair in the collection.

Making use of this second formulation we have the following definition of mapping. A *mapping* of a set A into a set B is a subset of $A \times B$ having the property that every element of A occurs in the first place of exactly one of the ordered pairs of the subset. We shall generally use the letters f and g, with or without subscripts, for mappings.

Let $A = \{a, b, c\}$, $B = \{\Delta, *\}$. Then each of the following subsets of $A \times B$ is a mapping of A into B.

$$f_1 = \{(a, \Delta), (b, \Delta), (c, \Delta)\};$$
$$f_2 = \{(a, *), (b, \Delta), (c, \Delta)\};$$
$$f_3 = \{(a, *), (b, *), (c, \Delta)\}.$$

There are others also. The following subsets of $A \times B$ are *not* mappings of A into B.

$$F_1 = \{(a, \Delta), (b, \Delta)\};$$
$$F_2 = \{(a, \Delta), (a, *), (b, *), (c, \Delta)\};$$
$$F_3 = \{(a, \Delta), (b, *)\}.$$

The following pictures depict the mappings designated f_1, f_2, f_3 above.

Similar pictures for the correspondences indicated by the sets F_1, F_2, F_3 are as follows.

By studying such pictures one should be able to gain a good intuitive feeling for what is meant by a mapping.

Note that a mapping of A into B is defined if we know the image of each a in A. Thus, the mapping f_1 defined on p. 6 could have been defined by the equations

$$f_1(a) = \Delta;$$
$$f_1(b) = \Delta;$$
$$f_1(c) = \Delta.$$

Each of these equalities indicates that the right side is the image of the element in the parentheses on the left side. The mapping f_3 defined on p. 6 can also be defined by stating

$$f_3(a) = *;$$
$$f_3(b) = *;$$
$$f_3(c) = \Delta.$$

Two mappings f and g of A into B are said to be *equal* if for all a in A it is true that $f(a) = g(a)$.

When f is a mapping of A into B we shall often write $A \xrightarrow{f} B$.

Remark: The word "function" is often used in place of "mapping." In this text, however, we use "mapping" exclusively.

● EXERCISES

1. For each of the three mappings f_1, f_2, f_3 give the image of a.

2. Enumerate all mappings from A into B when $A = \{a, b, c\}$, $B = \{\Delta, *\}$.

3. Let A be a set with n elements and B be a set with m elements. How many mappings of A into B are there?

4. Let $S = \{2, 6, 10, 14, 18, \cdots\}$, $T = \{1, 2, 3, 4, 5, \cdots\}$, and f be the rule which associates to each s in S the image $(\frac{1}{2})s$.
   (a) Is f a mapping of S into T?
   (b) What is $f(10)$?
   (c) If we enlarge S by the inclusion of the number 1, is f a mapping of S into T?
   (d) Compute $f(6), f(128)$.

(e) Replace T by a smaller set $\overline{T}$ such that f if a mapping of S into $\overline{T}$.

(f) Characterize all $\overline{T}$ which work in part (e).

(g) Replace S by $\{0, 2, 6, 10, 14, 18, \cdots\}$. Is f a mapping of this new S into T? If not, what is the simplest change you can make in T so that it becomes a mapping of S into T?

5. Which of the mappings f_1, f_2, f_3 would you like to call "onto" mappings?

I.3. Mappings and Operations

In the last section we introduced the notion of a mapping of one set into a second set. In the examples of mappings it will be noted that not every element of the second set is necessarily an image of some element of the first set. For instance, in the following mapping of A into B, where $f(a) = 2a$, only the even num-

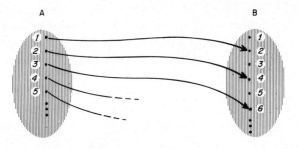

bers in B are images. In general, if $A \xrightarrow{f} B$, then the set of images is called the *range* of the mapping f. In the above example the range of f is the collection of even natural numbers.

When the range of f, $A \xrightarrow{f} B$, is all of B we say that f is a mapping of A *onto* B. (Note, however, that when we say f is a mapping of A into B we do not intend to imply that the mapping is not onto.) In Section I.2 the mappings f_2 and f_3 are onto mappings, and the mapping f_1 has the range $\{\Delta\}$.

We often wish to associate with certain pairs of elements of a set another element of the same set. For instance, let Z be the set

$\{1, 2, 3, \cdots\}$ of natural numbers. Then for purposes of addition we wish to associate with each pair of elements of Z another element of Z called their *sum*. We can think of this in the following way. A machine is given, which we call $+$, which yields an element of Z for each two elements of Z fed into it (see below). Thus, if 5 is fed in at the upper left and 3 is fed in at the upper right, we get 8, that is $5 + 3$, at the bottom. We can think of the machine as "operating" on the numbers a and b to give the number $a + b$. This example affords us with a method for defining an *operation* in a set S.

Suppose we denote by Θ a machine such that when certain elements of the set S are fed into it (see below) the machine produces an element of S at the bottom. [It may happen that the

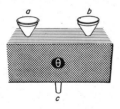

machine will not accept a in the left funnel and b in the right funnel for some pairs (a, b). This will be discussed later.] Examining the above we see that we can regard an operation Θ as a mapping of a subset D of $S \times S$ into S. The subset D will contain (a, b) if and only if the machine will accept a in the left funnel and b in the right funnel. It then produces $\Theta((a, b))$, the image of (a, b) under Θ. For convenience we shall write $a\Theta b$ rather than $\Theta((a, b))$. When the machine will accept every element of S in either funnel we call the set S *closed* with respect to the operation Θ. Thus, the set Z of natural numbers is closed with respect to the operation of addition.

Formally, we have the following:

Let D by a subset of $S \times S$. Then any mapping of D into S is called an *operation* in S. If the set D is $S \times S$, then S is *closed with respect to* the operation. (We also say that the operation is *closed*.) The set D is called the *domain* of the operation. The *range* of the operation is the set of image elements of D under Θ.

● EXAMPLES

(a) Let S be the collection $\{1, 2, 3, 5, 7, 9, 11, 13, \cdots\}$. Then $S \times S$ consists of all ordered pairs (a, b), where both a and b are positive odd integers, along with all ordered pairs of the forms $(2, a)$ and $(a, 2)$, where a is a positive odd integer, along with the pair $(2, 2)$. Let D be the collection of elements of $S \times S$ having exactly one 2; that is, $D = \{(1, 2), (3, 2), (5, 2), \cdots, (2, 1), (2, 3), (2, 5), \cdots\}$. If we define, for (a, b) in D, $a \Theta b$ to be $a + b$; that is, Θ maps (a, b) in D into $a + b$ in S, then Θ is an operation in S. We have $5 \Theta 2 = 7, 2 \Theta 17 = 19$. The domain of Θ is the set D, and the range is the set $\{3, 5, 7, 9, 11, \cdots\}$. The set S is not closed with respect to Θ, since D is not $S \times S$.

Sometimes there is a convenient tabular method for defining an operation in S. We illustrate by means of the next example.

(b) Let
$$S = \{a, b, c, d\};$$
$$D = \{(a, b), (a, c), (a, d), (b, c), (b, d)\};$$
$$\Theta = \{((a, b), a), ((a, c), a), ((a, d), a),$$
$$((b, c), b), ((b, d), b)\}.$$

We claim that Θ is an operation in S. To check this, we need only verify that D is a subset of $S \times S$ and Θ is a mapping of D into S. Further, we claim Θ is not closed, since $D \neq S \times S$.

In accordance with the above conventions, the following three statements are equivalent.

   (i) $((a, b), a)$ is in Θ;

  (ii) $\Theta((a, b)) = a$;

 (iii) $a \Theta b = a$.

In the sequel we shall almost always use the form given in (iii). Thus, the assertion that $\Theta = \{((a, b), a), ((a, c), a), ((a, d), a), ((b, c), b), ((b, d), b)\}$ is equivalent to the assertions

$a\Theta b = a,$ $b\Theta c = b,$
$a\Theta c = a,$ $b\Theta d = b.$
$a\Theta d = a,$

Θ	a	b	c	d
a		a	a	a
b			b	b
c				
d				

This last method of defining Θ can be put in tabular form, as on the right. If $\alpha\Theta\beta$ is defined for α and β in S, then we place $\alpha\Theta\beta$ in the intersection of the row corresponding to α and the column corresponding to β. Hence this example is completely determined by specifying S and the table for Θ.

(c) Let $S = \{1, -1, i, -i\}$, where i is an arbitrary symbol. Let Θ be defined by the following table. The set S is closed relative to Θ.

(If you are familiar with complex numbers, you can interpret Θ to be ordinary multiplication of complex numbers and i to be one of the complex square roots of -1.)

Θ	1	-1	i	$-i$
1	1	-1	i	$-i$
-1	-1	1	$-i$	i
i	i	$-i$	-1	1
$-i$	$-i$	i	1	-1

● EXERCISES

1. Is it possible to enlarge D in example (a), p. 10, by adding more elements of S × S to it if the Θ, as defined, is to be an operation in S with domain the enlarged D?

2. Let $S = \{1, 2, 4, 6, 8, 10, 12, \cdots\}$, and let D be an unknown subset of S × S. Find the largest subset D of S × S such that S is closed with respect to the operation Θ for which $a\Theta b = a + b$ for each (a, b) in D.

3. Let $S = \{0, 1, 2, 3, 4\}$, and define $a\Theta b$ for (a, b) in S × S to be the remainder obtained when $a + b$ is divided by 5. Show that Θ is an operation in S. Is S closed with respect to Θ?

4. Let $S = \{0, 1, 2, 3, \cdots, p - 1\}$, where p is a natural number. Find an operation in S with respect to which S is closed.

5. Let $S = Z = \{1, 2, 3, 4, \cdots\}$. Show that ordinary addition of numbers in Z can be conceived as an operation in Z and that Z is closed with respect to this operation.

6. Repeat the preceding problem for multiplication.

7. What characteristic feature of an operation table will betray the closure or nonclosure of an operation?

8. (a) Let $S = \{a, b, c, d\}$. Show that there are 5^{16} different operations definable in S.

(b) How many of the 5^{16} operations possible in S are closed?

(c) Generalize parts (a) and (b) to a set S with n elements.

9. In example (c), p. 11, write Θ as a subset of $(S \times S) \times S$.

10. Specify the ranges and domains of the operations in examples (a) through (c).

I.4. Relations يض

In everyday life the word "relation" is used in a slightly more special way than it is used in mathematics. In order to introduce the idea behind the mathematical use of the word we shall give a perhaps unusual but meaningful way of thinking about the relation "brother of."

Let S be the collection of all living or dead male humans, and let T be the collection of all living or dead humans. Then the collection of all ordered pairs (a, b) where a is or was a brother of b is a natural kind of collection to consider in connection with the relation "brother of." Given this collection we can answer such questions as: Did John have a brother?, How many brothers does Jane have?, and so on. We shall call this collection itself the relation "brother of." Similarly, we can define other everyday relations in terms of certain collections of ordered pairs. The "brother of" relation is a subset of $S \times T$. Certain other subsets of $S \times T$ will be distinguished by familiar terms, such as "father of," "husband of," and so on. On the other hand, certain subsets of $S \times T$ will have no familiar names attached and will therefore not define relations in the ordinary sense. This is where the word "relation" takes on a wider meaning in mathematics. We shall call *every* subset of S × T a relation (*on S to T*). Thus, if S and T are arbitrary sets, then a relation on S to T is a subset of S × T, and every subset of S × T is a relation on S to T.

We have already met some special relations in Section I.2. They were called mappings. Clearly, all mappings from A into B, being subsets of A × B, are relations on A to B. However, not all relations on A to B are mappings. [Remember, to be a mapping, a relation must contain one and *only* one element (*a*, *b*) for each *a* in A.]

When R is a relation on S to T and (*s*, *t*) is in R we shall write *sRt*. Thus, "*sRt*" means "(*s*, *t*) is in R."

A relation on S to S is called a *relation* in S. A certain kind of relation in a set which plays a rather dominant role in the following pages is the *linear order relation*. A *linear order relation* R in S is a relation in S which satisfies the following:

2 (i) for no *s* is *sRs* true; irreversible law

3 (ii) for *s*, *s'* distinct elements of S, either *sRs'* or *s'Rs*;

4 (iii) if *sRs'* and *s'Rs''*, then *sRs''*. transitive law

For example, put S = {Δ, ∗, □, O}, and take R = {(Δ, ∗), (Δ, O), (Δ, □), (∗, O), (∗, □), (O, □)}. Thus, ΔR∗, ΔRO, ΔR□, ∗RO, ∗R□, OR□. Since each of ΔRΔ, ∗R∗, □R□, and ORO is false, R has the first property of a linear order relation. You should check to see that the other two properties also hold for R. Therefore R is a linear order relation in S.

If for this example we string out the elements of S in the order

$$\Delta * O \square,$$

then we see that *sRs'* if and only if *s* is to the left of *s'*. For instance, ΔR□ and Δ *is* to the left of □. This is no accident. Indeed, if we string out these elements in any other order, then that string will "induce" a linear order relation in S. We illustrate this by stringing the elements of the above set S in the order

$$\square * O \Delta$$

and defining R̄ such that *sR̄s'* if and only if *s* is to the left of *s'* in

this ordering. Then
$$\square \bar{R}*, \ \square \bar{R}O, \ \square \bar{R}\Delta, \ *\bar{R}O, \ *\bar{R}\Delta, \ O\bar{R}\Delta,$$
and direct checking will reveal $\bar{R}$ to be a linear order relation in S.

It is not difficult to see that each listing of the elements of S in a horizontal line yields a linear order relation in this same way. Conversely, if we have a linear order relation defined in a set S, this gives rise to such a listing of the elements of the set.

Since four objects can be arranged in $4 \cdot 3 \cdot 2 \cdot 1 = 24$ ways on a line, there are exactly 24 distinct linear order relations in the above set S.

As another example, consider Z, the set $\{1, 2, 3, \cdots\}$ of natural numbers, and define the relation R in Z to be the collection of all (a, b) where $a < b$. Then R is a linear order relation in Z, since:

(i) for no a is $a < a$;

(ii) for $a \neq b$ either $a < b$ or $b < a$;

(iii) if $a < b$ and $b < c$, then $a < c$.

This linear order relation strings the set out in its natural ordering: $1, 2, 3, 4, 5, \cdots$.

● EXERCISES

1. Let S be the collection of all living or dead female humans and let T be the collection of all living or dead humans. Define two common relations on S to T.

2. Is $S \times T$ a relation on S to T? If S and T are finite collections, how many relations are there on S to T?

3. Let $S = \{a, b, c\}$ and $R = \{(a, b), (b, c), (c, a)\}$. Is R a relation in S? Is R a linear order relation in S? If the answer to the last question is "no," which of the three properties for a linear order relation are violated?

4.* Show that if R is a linear order relation in S, then both sRs' and $s'Rs$ cannot hold. Conclude that if R is a linear order relation in S, then for any elements a, b in S one and only one of $aRb, a = b, bRa$ must hold. [The last property is referred to as "trichotomy" (With respect to R.)]

5. Find a relation in S = $\{a, b, c\}$ which satisfies the last two conditions but violates the first condition for a linear order relation.

6. Define three distinct linear order relations in the set S = $\{a, b, c, d, e\}$. For each of them string out the set S appropriately.

7. Discuss "relation tables" in connection with linear order relations.

I.5. Algebraic Systems

Two familiar operations defined in the collection $Z = \{1, 2, \cdots\}$ of natural numbers are addition and multiplication. A familiar relation is the "less than" relation. When we wish to think about the collection Z relative to both of these operations and this relation we shall speak of the *algebraic system* $(Z; +, \cdot ; <)$. If we wish to think about Z and its properties relative only to addition, we shall speak of the algebraic system $(Z; +)$. Thus, the system $(Z; +)$ has only one operation, namely, addition. In addition to these two algebraic systems involving Z there are the other familiar systems $(Z; \cdot)$, $(Z; +, \cdot)$, $(Z; +; <)$, $(Z; \cdot ; <)$, $(Z; ; <)$. Of course, we can introduce many operations other than $+$ and $\cdot$ into Z and speak of systems relative to these other operations. Similar remarks hold for relations.

In general, if S is a set in which we have defined a number of operations, say $\Theta_1, \cdots, \Theta_n$ and in which a number of relations $R_1, \cdots, R_m$ are defined, we can speak of the algebraic system $(S; \Theta_1, \cdots, \Theta_n; R_1, \cdots, R_m)$. (It is also possible that no operations or no relations appear.) We shall call S the *set of the algebraic system*. If S is closed with respect to the operation Θ_i, then we say that the system $(S; \Theta_1, \cdots, \Theta_n; R_1, \cdots, R_m)$ is closed with respect to Θ_i. Similarly, this system is said to be linearly ordered relative to R_i if S is linearly ordered with respect to R_i.

It is clear that in general there are a great many operations and relations in S. It is also clear that in a given discussion most of these operations and relations are of little interest. The introduction of algebraic systems enables us to designate, along with a set, those operations and relations which we are to regard as relevant in a given discussion.

As a further example, let A be the set of all (a, b) in Z $\times$ Z for which $a > b$. Define the operation Θ in Z with domain A by the equation $a\Theta b = X_{ab}$, where X_{ab} is the unique solution in Z of the equation $a = b + x$. Then $(Z; \Theta)$ is an algebraic system. This system is not closed with respect to Θ, since A $\neq$ Z $\times$ Z. Ordinarily we use the sign $-$ instead of Θ for this operation. Then, rather than $5\Theta 3 = 2$ we have $5 - 3 = 2$. Then $(Z; \Theta)$ becomes $(Z; -)$. (As already observed, Z is not closed with respect to $-$. This is one reason why Z is not satisfactory for many purposes.)

● EXERCISES

1. Let S $= \{1, -1, i, -i\}$. Construct a system $(S; \Theta; R_1, R_2)$ in such a way that the system is closed with respect to the operation Θ and is linearly ordered with respect to each of the two distinct relations R_1 and R_2. (In particular you could, if you wished, define Θ in such a way that $i\Theta i = -1$.)

2. Let S $= \{0, 1, 2, 3, 4, 5, 6\}$. Construct a system $(S; \Theta; R)$ which is closed with respect to Θ, and while not being linearly ordered with respect to R the relation R is to have the third of the three linear ordering properties.

3. Let I $= \{\cdots, -3, -2, -1, 0, 1, 2, 3, \cdots\}$, and consider the system $(I; \cdot)$ where $\cdot$ is the ordinary multiplication. Define a second operation, division ("inverse" of multiplication), along the lines carried out in defining subtraction in the example above. Is the resulting system $(I; \cdot, \div)$, where $\div$ is used for the division operation, closed with respect to division?

4. Keeping the definition of $a\Theta b$ given in the example above, show that for this example the domain of Θ in the system $(Z; \Theta)$ cannot be larger than A.

I.6. Isomorphic Systems

Sometimes we wish to investigate two algebraic systems, say $(S_1; \Theta_1)$ and $(S_2; \Theta_2)$. For purposes of economy, if not aesthetics, it behooves the investigator to decide whether or not the two systems are "essentially the same." If they are essentially the same, only one of them need be examined. It is the purpose of this section to give the conditions under which two systems are to be regarded as "essentially the same." We use the word *isomorphic* in this connection. For convenience we introduce the notion of a 1 to 1 mapping.

If f is a mapping of S onto T, then f is a *1 to 1 mapping* if no element of T is the image of more than one element of S.

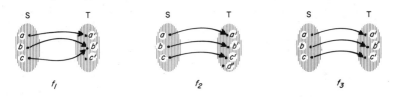

Now let $S^* = (S; \Theta)$, $T^* = (T; \Theta')$ be two algebraic systems. Suppose there exists a map f of S onto T such that:

(i) f is 1 to 1;

(ii) when one of $a\Theta b$ and $f(a)\Theta' f(b)$ is defined, so is the other (here a and b are in S);

(iii) $f(a\Theta b) = f(a)\Theta' f(b)$, when (a, b) is in the domain of Θ.

Then f is called an *isomorphism* of S^* with T^* (and S^* and T^* are called *isomorphic*). (Note that if S^*, T^* are closed with respect to Θ, Θ', respectively, then property (ii) is automatically satisfied.) When S^*, T^* are isomorphic we write $S^* \cong T^*$. If f is an isomorphism of S^*, T^*, we write $S^* \overset{f}{\cong} T^*$.

To make clear the third property, we draw a picture. Let a, b be in S such that $a\Theta b$ is defined in S. Then $f(a)$, $f(b)$ are in T, and by property (ii), $f(a)\Theta' f(b)$ is defined in T. Property (iii) says that the image, $f(a\Theta b)$, of $a\Theta b$ must be $f(a)\Theta' f(b)$.

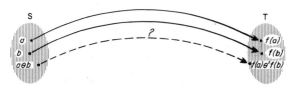

● EXAMPLES

(a) Consider the following two systems.

(S; Θ), where   (S'; Θ'), where
S = {a, b, c, d}   S' = {1, −1, i, −1}

Θ	a	b	c	d
a	a	b	c	d
b	b	a	d	c
c	c	d	b	a
d	d	c	a	b

Θ'	1	−1	i	−i
1	1	−1	i	−i
−1	−1	1	−i	i
i	i	−i	−1	1
−i	−i	i	1	−1

We claim that these systems are isomorphic. To substantiate this, we should prove that there exists a mapping f of S onto S' which satisfies properties (i), (ii), and (iii), p. 17. We shall do even more — we shall actually exhibit such a mapping f.

Define f by

$$f(a) = 1,$$
$$f(b) = -1,$$
$$f(c) = i,$$
$$f(d) = -i.$$

Clearly, f is a 1 to 1 mapping of S onto S', so property (i) holds. Since each system is closed relative to its operation, property (ii) holds automatically. Examining the operation tables we see that property (iii) also holds. We check one instance of property (iii):

$$f(c\Theta d) = f(a) = 1;$$
$$f(c)\Theta' f(d) = i\Theta'(-i) = 1;$$

and therefore

$$f(c\Theta d) = f(c)\Theta' f(d).$$

(b) Let S; Θ) be such that S = {0, 1, 2} and Θ is the operation mapping (s, s') onto the remainder of $s + s'$ on division by 3. The operation table for Θ is shown below on the left. Let

$(\overline{S}; \overline{\Theta})$ be such that $\overline{S} = \{a, b, c\}$ and $\overline{\Theta}$ is the operation whose table is shown below on the right. Then $(S; \Theta) \overset{f}{\cong} (\overline{S}; \overline{\Theta})$, where $f(0) = a, f(1) = b, f(2) = c$.

Θ	0	1	2
0	0	1	2
1	1	2	0
2	2	0	1

$\overline{\Theta}$	a	b	c
a	a	b	c
b	b	c	a
c	c	a	b

(c) Let R^+ denote the set of positive real numbers, and let R denote the set of all real numbers. Then, if $\cdot$ and $+$ are the ordinary multiplication and addition operations, we have

$$(R^+; \cdot) \cong (R; +).$$

That is, the positive real numbers under ordinary multiplication are isomorphic with all real numbers under ordinary addition. To see this, we can choose f to be any one of the (infinitely many) logarithm functions. For example, let $f(r) = \log r$ for r in R^+, where "log" stands for the base 10 logarithm. Then $(R^+; \cdot) \overset{f}{\cong} (R; +)$. (Since f could also be the "natural logarithm," or any other logarithm, this example shows that there may be several different isomorphisms between two algebraic systems.)

(d) Let $S = \{a, b\}$, $T = \{0, 1\}$, and define Θ, Θ' in S, T, respectively, by the following tables.

Θ	a	b
a	a	a
b	a	b

Θ'	0	1
0	0	0
1	1	1

We claim that the systems $(S; \Theta)$, $(T; \Theta')$ are *not* isomorphic. We prove this by showing that every 1 to 1 mapping of S onto T fails to satisfy the third property of an isomorphic mapping. In this example there are exactly two 1 to 1 mappings of S onto T. They are f_1 and f_2, where $f_1(a) = 0, f_1(b) = 1; f_2(a) = 1, f_2(b) = 0$. To show the third property of an isomorphic mapping is false, we observe its failure in a single instance—for each of f_1, f_2:

$$f_1(b\Theta a) = f_1(a) = 0 \neq 1 = 1\Theta'0 = f_1(b)\Theta'f_1(a);$$
$$f_2(b\Theta a) = f_2(a) = 1 \neq 0 = 0\Theta'1 = f_2(b)\Theta'f_2(a).$$

We turn our attention to the definition of isomorphism when applied to systems of the form $(S; ; R)$ and $(\bar{S}; ; \bar{R})$. Indeed, we say that $(S; ; R)$ is isomorphic to $(\bar{S}; ; \bar{R})$, and write $(\bar{S}; ; \bar{R}) \cong (S; ; R)$, if there is a mapping of S onto $\bar{S}$ such that
  (i) f is 1 to 1;
  (ii) $s_1 R s_2$ if and only if $f(s_1)\bar{R}f(s_2)$.

● E X A M P L E S (continued)

  (e) Let $S = \{a, b, c, d\}$ and $\bar{S} = \{\Delta, *, O, \Box\}$. Define R, $\bar{R}$ in S, $\bar{S}$, respectively, as follows:

$$aRb, aRd, cRb, cRc;$$
$$\Delta\bar{R}*, \Delta\bar{R}\Box, O\bar{R}*, O\bar{R}O.$$

Then $(S; ; R) \cong (\bar{S}; ; \bar{R})$, where $f(a) = \Delta, f(b) = *, f(c) = O, f(d) = \Box$.

  (f) Let $S = \{*, \Delta\}$ and $\bar{S} = \{4, 5\}$. Define R, $\bar{R}$ in S, $\bar{S}$, respectively, as follows:

$$*R*, *R\Delta, \Delta R*;$$
$$4\bar{R}4, 5\bar{R}5, 5\bar{R}4.$$

Then the systems $(S; ; R), (\bar{S}; ; \bar{R})$ are *not* isomorphic. To prove this, we show that every 1 to 1 mapping of S onto $\bar{S}$ fails to be an isomorphism. In this example there are exactly two 1 to 1 mappings of S onto $\bar{S}$. They are f_1 and f_2, where

$$f_1(*) = 4, \quad f_1(\Delta) = 5;$$
$$f_2(*) = 5, \quad f_2(\Delta) = 4.$$

Since $\Delta R\Delta$ is false, but $f_1(\Delta)\bar{R}f_1(\Delta)$ is true, the mapping f_1 is not an isomorphism. Since $\Delta R*$ is true, but $f_2(\Delta)\bar{R}f_2(*)$ is false, the mapping f_2 is not an isomorphism.

  In general, the systems $(S; \Theta_1, \cdots, \Theta_n; R_1, \cdots, R_m)$ and

$(\bar{S}; \bar{\Theta}_1, \cdots, \bar{\Theta}_n; \bar{R}_1, \cdots, \bar{R}_m)$ are isomorphic if there exists a mapping f of S onto $\bar{S}$ such that

$$(S; \Theta_i) \cong (\bar{S}; \bar{\Theta}_i)$$

and

$$(S; ; R_j) \cong (\bar{S}; ; \bar{R}_j)$$

for all $i = 1, 2, \cdots, n$ and $j = 1, 2, \cdots, m$. (The mapping f must be the same for all of the pairs Θ_i, $\bar{\Theta}_i$ and R_j, $\bar{R}_j$.)

● EXERCISES

1. (a) Complete the proof of property (iii) for example (a), p. 18.

(b) What property of the logarithm functions guarantees the assertions made in example (c), p. 19?

2. Consider the proposition: If f is a mapping of S onto S, then f is a 1 to 1 mapping.

(a) Prove this proposition when S is a finite set.

(b) Show that the proposition is not true in general.

3. Let $S = \{0, 1, 2, 3, 4\}$, $\bar{S} = \{a, b, c, d, e\}$, and Θ be an operation defined in S by $s\Theta s' = 3$ for all s, s' in S. Define an operation $\bar{\Theta}$ in $\bar{S}$ such that $(S; \Theta) \cong (\bar{S}; \bar{\Theta})$. Exhibit an f giving rise to the isomorphism.

4. Let S be the collecton of all numbers of the form $m + n\sqrt{3}$, where m and n are integers. Define the mapping f of S into S by the equation $f(m + n\sqrt{3}) = m - n\sqrt{3}$ for all integers m and n. Show that f is an isomorphism of $(S; +, \cdot)$ with itself (the $+$ and $\cdot$ are the ordinary addition and multiplication operations). (Such an isomorphism of a set with itself is called an *automorphism*.)

5. Let $S = Z = \{1, 2, 3, 4, \cdots\}$, $T = \{\omega, 1, 2, 3, \cdots\}$. Let $<$ be the usual less-than relation in S. Let the relation R in T consist of all pairs (a, b) where a and b are positive integers with $a < b$ along with all pairs (a, ω), where a is a positive integer. We know that $(S; ; <)$ is linearly ordered with respect to $<$. Show that $(T; ; R)$ is linearly ordered with respect to R. Show also that $(S ; ; <)$ is *not* isomorphic with $(T; ; R)$ even though there *do* exist 1 to 1 mappings from S onto T.

6.* Prove the following propositions.

(i) $(S; \Theta) \cong (S; \Theta)$.

(ii) If $(S; \Theta) \cong (S'; \Theta')$, then $(S'; \Theta') \cong (S; \Theta)$.

(iii) If $(S; \Theta) \cong (S'; \Theta')$ and $(S'; \Theta') \cong (S''; \Theta'')$, then $(S; \Theta) \cong (S''; \Theta'')$.

I.7. Properties of Operations

Let Θ be an operation under which S is closed. Then we call Θ:

commutative if $s\Theta s' = s'\Theta s$ for all s, s' in S;

associative if $s\Theta(s'\Theta s'') = (s\Theta s')\Theta s''$ for all s, s', s'' in S.

In terms of the machines in section III, these properties of operations can be expressed by the following pictures.

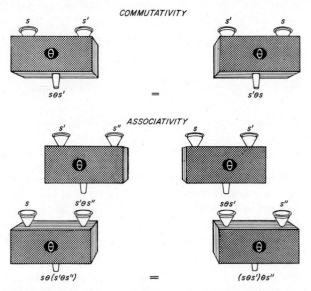

If Θ and Θ' are two operations under which S is closed, then we say that Θ is *distributive* over $\bar{\Theta}$ if $s\Theta(s'\bar{\Theta}s'') = (s\Theta s')\bar{\Theta}(s\Theta s'')$ and $(s'\bar{\Theta}s'')\Theta s = (s'\Theta s)\bar{\Theta}(s''\Theta s)$ for all s, s', s'' in S.

Let Θ be an operation under which S is closed. If s_0 is an element of S and if

$$s\Theta s_0 = s_0\Theta s = s$$

for all s in S, we call s_0 a Θ-*identity*.

● EXAMPLES

(a) Consider the system $(Z; +, \cdot)$. This system is closed with respect to the operations $+$ and $\cdot$. Both of these operations are commutative and associative. The operation $\cdot$ is distributive over $+$, since $a(b + c) = ab + ac$ for all a, b, c, in Z. There is no additive identity (that is, $+$-identity) but 1 is a multiplicative identity (that is, a $\cdot$-identity).

(b) Consider the system $(Z; \Theta)$, where Θ is defined in such a way that $a\Theta b = b$ for all a, b in Z. Clearly, the system is closed with respect to Θ. But Θ is not commutative, since if $a \neq b$, then $a\Theta b$ (equal to b) and $b\Theta a$ (equal to a) are distinct. We see that Θ is associative, since for all a, b, c in Z, $a\Theta(b\Theta c) = a\Theta c = c = b\Theta c = (a\Theta b)\Theta c$. If there were a Θ-identity, say a, we would have to have $b\Theta a = b$ for all b in Z. But by definition of Θ, $b\Theta a = a$ for all b in Z. Hence there is no Θ-identity in this system.

(c) Consider $(Z; \Theta)$, where Θ is defined in such a way that $a\Theta b = (\max(a, b))^{\min(a, b)}$ for all a, b in Z. [We define $\max(a, b)$ to be the larger of a and b if $a \neq b$, and to be a if $a = b$. A similar definition holds for $\min(a, b)$.] The system is closed with respect to this operation. Also, since $\max(a, b) = \max(b, a)$ and $\min(a, b) = \min(b, a)$, the operation is commutative. However, Θ is not associative, as can be seen by the example $(2\Theta3)\Theta4 = 3^2\Theta4 = 9^4$, $2\Theta(3\Theta4) = 2\Theta4^3 = 64^2$. The number 1 is a Θ-identity, since $1\Theta a = a\Theta 1 = a$ for all a in Z.

● EXERCISES

1. How can we determine from an operation table whether or not the operation defined by the table is commutative?

2. Let Θ be defined in Z in such a way that $a\Theta b = a^b$ for all a, b in Z. Show that $(Z; \Theta)$ is closed with respect to Θ but that Θ is neither commutative nor associative. Is there a Θ-identity?

3. Prove the following for example (c) above:
(i) If one of a, b, c equals 1, then $(a\Theta b)\Theta c = a\Theta(b\Theta c)$.

(ii) $(a\Theta b)\Theta a = a\Theta(b\Theta a)$.

[*Hint:* no computation is necessary to prove (ii).]

4. Prove that 1 is the only Θ-identity in the system of example (c).

5. Let 2^S where S is a set, designate the collection of all subsets of S (including the empty set, designated Θ). (This collection 2^S is called the *power set of* S.) Define two operations, denoted by $\cup$, $\cap$, in 2^S as follows:

A $\cup$ B is that subset of S which contains all those elements of S which are contained in at least one of the sets A and B;

A $\cap$ B is that subset of S which contains all elements of S which are in both sets A and B.

By definition, the system $(2^S; \cup, \cap)$ is closed with respect to $\cup$ and $\cap$. Prove that both of these operations are commutative and associative and that each is distributive over the other. Is there either a $\cup$-identity or an $\cap$-identity? If so prove it. (The operations $\cup$, $\cap$ are called *union* and *intersection*, respectively.)

6.* Prove that any system $(S; \Theta)$ has at most one Θ-identity.

I.8. Extensions

Throughout the text we encounter algebraic systems which have many desirable properties, but which are yet not quite satisfactory for our purposes because they lack certain other desired properties. For this reason it is desirable to have a method which can be used to make a system "grow." The process of growth should not proceed in such a way that old desirable properties are lost; it should take place in such a way that new desirable properties are gained. This is necessarily somewhat vague. In this section we wish to indicate an abstract notion which can be used in lieu of the growth process described above. To obtain a larger system than the one in hand, we can make the present system grow, *or* we can seek an "extension system" in which the present system has an isomorphic replica. We have adopted the second alternative. We now say precisely what we mean by an extension of the algebraic system, $(S; \Theta)$:

$(\bar{S}; \bar{\Theta})$ is an extension of $(S; \Theta)$ if there is
a subset S′ of $\bar{S}$ such that $(S'; \Theta) \cong (S; \bar{\Theta})$.

Pictorially, we have the following:

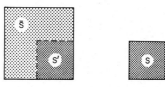

$$(\text{S}'; \bar{\theta}) \cong (\text{S}; \theta)$$

In general, $(\bar{S}; \bar{\Theta}_1, \cdots, \bar{\Theta}_n; \bar{R}_1, \cdots, \bar{R}_m)$ is an extension of $(S; \Theta_1, \cdots, \Theta_n; R_1, \cdots, R_m)$ if there is a subset S' of $\bar{S}$ such that $(S'; \bar{\Theta}_1, \cdots, \bar{\Theta}_n; \bar{R}_1, \cdots, \bar{R}_m) \cong (S; \Theta_1, \cdots, \Theta_n; R_1, \cdots, R_m)$.

● EXAMPLES

(a) Let $S = \{1, -1\}$ and $\bar{S} = \{a, b, c, d\}$. Define Θ, $\bar{\Theta}$ in S, $\bar{S}$, respectively, by the following tables.

Θ	1	-1
1	1	-1
-1	-1	1

$\bar{\Theta}$	a	b	c	d
a	a	b	c	d
b	b	c	d	a
c	c	d	a	b
d	d	a	b	c

If we take $S' = \{a, c\}$, then $(S; \Theta) \overset{f}{\cong} (S'; \bar{\Theta})$ when

$$f(1) = a,$$
$$f(-1) = c.$$

Therefore $(\bar{S}; \bar{\Theta})$ is an extension of $(S; \Theta)$. [It is of interest to note that the equation $x\Theta x = -1$ is not solvable in $(S; \Theta)$, but the corresponding equation $x\bar{\Theta}x = c$ is solvable in $(\bar{S}; \bar{\Theta})$. This suggests renaming a and c of $\bar{S}$ 1 and -1, respectively. Using these new names we have:

$$\bar{S} = \{1, b, -1, d\}$$

$\bar\Theta$	1	b	-1	d
1	1	b	-1	d
b	b	-1	d	1
-1	-1	d	1	b
d	d	1	b	-1

The system now even "looks" like an extension of $(S; \Theta)$. We note that $x\bar\Theta x = -1$ is solvable in $\bar{S}$—it even has two solutions. (This example is due to Dorothy Christensen.)]

(b) Let J be the collection of all integers. Then $(J; +; <)$ is an extension of $(Z; +; <)$, where Z is, as usual, the collection of natural numbers.

(c) Let R be the set of real numbers. Then $(R; +; <)$ is an extension of $(J; +; <)$.

● EXERCISES

1. Find a sequence of subsets $M_1, M_2, M_3, \cdots$ of Z such that each M_i contains the next following M_{i+1} and such that $(M_1; +)$ is an extension of $(M_2; +)$ which is an extension of $(M_3; +)$, and so on. Furthermore, each system is to be closed with respect to $+$.

2. Show that if $(S''; \Theta'')$ is an extension of $(S'; \Theta')$ and $(S'; \Theta')$ is an extension of $(S; \Theta)$, then $(S''; \Theta'')$ is an extension of $(S; \Theta)$.

II The Natural Numbers

In Chapter I we introduced the basic algebraic notions we shall use throughout the text. In presenting these notions we often made use of the sets of integers or rational numbers or of real numbers. None of these sets played an essential role in the development of the main ideas of the chapter; they were used only in an illustrative capacity.

In this chapter we lay down the ground rules for our development of the real numbers—starting with the natural numbers. In later chapters we shall systematically discuss the rational numbers and the real numbers, basing our analyses upon the beginnings given in this chapter. The discussion in this chapter starts as if the reader had never heard of the natural numbers.

II.1. Axioms for the Natural Numbers

We begin with a nonempty collection of objects which are called *natural numbers*. We denote this collection by Z. In this collection are defined two operations and a relation. The operations are called *addition* and *multiplication* and are symbolized $+$ and $\cdot$, respectively. The relation is a linear ordering relation and is denoted by $<$. Thus, we are dealing with an algebraic system $(Z; +, \cdot; <)$.

The system $(Z; +, \cdot; <)$ is nothing more than the collection of natural numbers with the usual rules of adding and multiplying and with the usual ordering. You should not forget this. Nevertheless, you should use this realization only as a guide to your reasoning. We are going to list several axioms that the system $(Z; +, \cdot; <)$ is to satisfy. Any properties of the system which we wish to use will have to be established on the basis of this list of axioms.

That the natural numbers, in their usual sense, satisfy these axioms is intuitively clear upon a little reflection, even though some of the axioms may at first seem strange. It is not so clear that any collection of "things" satisfying the axioms will be just like (that is, will be isomorphic to) the natural numbers in their usual sense. Indeed, we could not prove any such theorem without defining carefully just what is meant by "the natural numbers in their usual sense." Our collection of axioms is to serve as such a definition.

In view of our above remarks, if a conflict arises between "the natural numbers in their usual sense" and "the natural numbers as the collection Z in the algebraic system $(Z; +, \cdot ; <)$ satisfying the given axioms," we must always decide in favor of the latter view.

The axioms are as follows. (Note that we generally write $a \cdot b$ as ab, suppressing the dot.)

    (i) $a + b$, $a \cdot b$ *are defined for all* a, b (system is closed with respect to $+$ and $\cdot$).

    (ii) (a) $a < a$ *is false for all* a;

        (b) $a < b$ *or* $a = b$ *or* $b < a$ *for all* a, b;

        (c) $a < b$ *and* $b < c$ *implies* $a < c$ *for all* a, b, c;

        ($<$ is a linear ordering relation).

    (iii) (a) $a + b = b + a$ *for all* a, b;

        (b) $ab = ba$ *for all* a, b;

        ($+$ and $\cdot$ are commutative).

    (iv) (a) $(a + b) + c = a + (b +)$ *for all* a, b, c;

        (b) $(ab)c = a(bc)$ *for all* a, b, c.

        ($+$ and $\cdot$ are associative).

    (v) $a(b + c) = ab + ac$ *for all* a, b, c ($\cdot$ is distributive over $+$).

    (vi) (a) *If* $a < b$, *there is a unique* c *such that* $a + c = b$;

        (b) $a < a + b$ *for all* a, b.

    (vii) (a) $a < b$ *implies* $a + c < b + c$ *for all* a, b, c;

        (b) $a < b$ *implies* $ac < bc$ *for all* a, b, c.

(viii) (*The least integer principle.*) *Every nonempty collection of natural numbers has a smallest element.* [In view of (viii) the collection Z has a smallest number. (Throughout this chapter the word "number" means "natural number.") Denote this number by 1. Then $1 < a$ for a in Z and $a \neq 1$. This number 1 appears in the next and last axiom.]

(ix) $1 \cdot a = a$ *for all* a (existence of a $\cdot$ -identity).

Although we do not list them as axioms we also assume the following properties for the equality relation:

$$\text{when } a = b \text{ then for all } c,$$
$$a + c = b + c,$$
$$ac = bc.$$

II.2. Some Consequences

In this section we shall prove several consequences of the axioms. These consequences will, in general, be quite familiar properties of the "whole numbers." That this is so should be very welcome; however, this fact is no substitute for proofs.

For the mathematician, an original discovery or invention comes about by rather strange thought processes and is not necessarily a logical consequence of other related thoughts passing through his mind at the same time. Ordinarily we do not think logically. However, once the discovery is made the result must be proved. This is another facet of mathematics: after a theorem has been divined it must be demonstrated.

Even here there are no set patterns of procedure. We try this and that. We guess. We try to generalize the result in order to make the proof easier. We try special cases to see if any insight can be gained in this way. Finally—who knows just how—a proof is obtained. How should it be written? Historically? If so, it will probably be unreadable, owing to verbosity. Logically? If so, it will probably be quite difficult to "understand." However, when written logically it will generally be easy to "follow" and will take the least space.

We shall usually make use of the logical presentation, even though it often necessitates presenting a proof in precisely the reverse order in which it was discovered. This is unfortunate, and it causes psychological complications that are not easily overcome. Nevertheless, it seems the best of a bad bargain, and it is here where a teacher is most useful to the student in pointing out the reasons behind the proofs. Understand carefully each theorem before reading the proof. Then scan, don't study yet, the proof, trying to grasp the key idea (or ideas), and see if a picture of the proof comes into the mind. Only after seeing the proof as a whole should the details be allowed to obtrude. (Incidentally, when one becomes quite familiar with this process he finds that after "understanding" the *idea* of a proof he can construct his own details easier than he can read somebody else's.)

With these remarks we proceed to the first lemma. If you do not see the necessity of proving this lemma, return to the beginning of the chapter and reread Section I up to the axioms.

LEMMA 1.   *Let c be a natural number. Then there is no natural number s such that $c < s < c + 1$.*

Proof: Suppose that for some c and s we do have $c < s < c + 1$. We shall show this supposition to be false by deriving from it a contradiction. From axiom (vi)(a) there are numbers a and b such that

$$c + a = s,$$
$$s + b = c + 1.$$

Hence, using axiom (iv)(a), we have

$$c + (a + b) = (c + a) + b = s + b = c + 1.$$

Since $<$ is a linear ordering relation we must have exactly one of

$$a + b < 1,$$
$$a + b = 1,$$
$$1 < a + b.$$

But $a + b < 1$ yields, using axiom (vii)(a),

$$c + (a + b) < c + 1,$$

which is in conflict with $c + (a + b) = c + 1$. Similarly, $1 < a + b$ yields

$$c + 1 < c + (a + b),$$

which is also in conflict with $c + (a + b) = c + 1$. Therefore, $a + b = 1$, and, by axiom (vi)(b), $a < 1$. If $a \neq 1$, this contradicts the definition of 1, and if $a = 1$, this contradicts axiom (ii)(a). In any event we have a contradiction. This completes the proof of the lemma.

By definition, 1 is the smallest natural number. Lemma 1 tells us that there is no natural number between 1 and $1 + 1$. Since every natural number not equal to $1 + 1$ must be less than $1 + 1$ or greater than $1 + 1$ and 1 is the only natural number less than $1 + 1$, we must conclude that the smallest natural number in the set Z with 1 removed is $1 + 1$. That is, $1 + 1$ is the second smallest natural number. We denote $1 + 1$ by the symbol 2.

By a similar argument, the smallest natural number in the set Z with 1 and 2 removed is $2 + 1$. We denote this number by the symbol 3.

Continuing, we develop the string

$$1, 2, 3, 4, 5, \cdots$$

such that

$$1 < 2 < 3 < 4 < 5 < \cdots$$

and such that no natural number appears between consecutive terms of this string.

It may be intuitively clear that every natural number will appear somewhere in this string $1, 2, 3, \cdots$. In fact, we hope that this does seem true. Our next lemma will, as a special case, prove that this is in fact the case.

We first introduce the symbols $>$, $\leq$, $\geq$. We write $a > b$ if and only if $b < a$; $a \leq b$ if and only if $a < b$ or $a = b$; $a \geq b$ if and only if $a > b$ or $a = b$.

LEMMA 2 (Principle of Mathematical Induction).   *Let* S *be a collection of natural numbers such that:*
   (i) *the number a is in* S; *and*
   (ii) *when b is in* S *and $b \geq a$ then $b + 1$ is in* S.
Then S *contains all natural numbers c such that $c \geq a$.*

Proof: Suppose (i) and (ii) hold. Let A be the (possibly empty) collection of numbers greater than a which are not in S. We shall show that the assumption that A is not empty leads to a contradiction. Therefore, A must be empty and all numbers greater than or equal to a are in S.

Thus, suppose A is not empty. Then by axiom (viii) there is a smallest number in A. Let it be $\bar{a}$. By the definition of A we know $a < \bar{a}$. This means that $1 < \bar{a}$. (Otherwise, $a \lessgtr \bar{a} \leq 1$, and the definition of 1 would be violated.) By axiom (vi)(a) there is a number c such that $1 + c = \bar{a}$. By Lemma 1 there are no numbers between c and $1 + c$. Hence, in as much as $a < \bar{a}$ we must have $a \leq c$. This means that c is in S (it is greater than or equal to a and smaller than the smallest number which is both greater than a and not in S). By condition (ii) we must then have $\bar{a} = c + 1$ in S. This is a contradiction. Hence, A is empty, and the lemma is proved.

Using this lemma we see that since the string

$$1, 2, 3, \cdots$$

contains 1 and contains $b + 1$ whenever it contains b, it must contain every natural number.

LEMMA 3. (*Archimedean principle.*) If a and b are natural numbers, there is a natural number n such that $b < an$.

Proof: If $a = 1$, then for $n = b + 1$ we have $b < b + 1 = a(b + 1) = an$. If $a \neq 1$, then there is a c such that $1 + c = a$. Hence, for $n = b$ we have $b < b + bc = b(1 + c) = ab = an$. This completes the proof.

We next define a^c, where a and c are natural numbers.

DEFINITION

$$a^1 = a$$
$$a^{b+1} = a^b \cdot a \text{ for } b \geq 1.$$

Using this definition we see that

$$a^2 = a^{1+1} = a^1 \cdot a = a \cdot a;$$
$$a^3 = a^{2+1} = a^2 \cdot a = (a \cdot a) \cdot a;$$
$$a^4 = a^{3+1} = a^3 \cdot a = ((a \cdot a) \cdot a) \cdot a$$

The question of whether this definition really does define a^c for all c can be settled quickly by using Lemma 2. Let S_a be the set of all c such that the definition does define a^c. Then since a^1 is defined to be a, we know that 1 is in S_a. Further, when b is in S_a we know that a^{b+1} is defined, since $a^{b+1} = a^b \cdot a$. Hence, $b + 1$ is in S_a. Thus, by Lemma 2, all natural numbers greater than or equal to 1 are in S_a. Since all natural numbers are greater than or equal to 1, this completes the proof.

We now give a lemma containing the so-called exponent laws.

LEMMA 4. *For any natural numbers a, b, c, d:*
(a) $a^c \cdot a^d = a^{c+d}$;
(b) $(a^c)^d = a^{cd}$.

Proof: (a) Let S be the collection of all d such that $a^c \cdot a^d = a^{c+d}$ for all c. Then 1 is in S, since $a^c \cdot a^1 = a^{c+1}$ and $a^1 = a$. Further, if b is in S, then $a^c \cdot a^b = a^{c+b}$, and therefore $a^{c+(b+1)} = a^{(c+b)+1} = a^{c+b} \cdot a = (a^c \cdot a^b) \cdot a = a^c \cdot (a^b \cdot a) = a^c \cdot a^{b+1}$. Hence, when b is in S so is $b + 1$. By Lemma 2 then, S contains all natural numbers.

(b) The proof is left as exercise 6, p. 34.

For further information about the logic of mathematical induction we refer the reader to the article "On Mathematical Induction," by Leon Henkin, *American Mathematical Monthly*, **67**, 1960, pp. 323–338.

● EXERCISES

1.* Prove that:
(a) $a + c < b + c$ implies $a < b$;
(b) $a + c = b + c$ implies $a = b$.
[*Hint:* For (a) show that $a = b$, $b < a$ are incompatible with $a + c < b + c$.]

2. Prove that:
(a) $ac < bc$ implies $a < b$;
(b) $ac = bc$ implies $a = b$.

3. Show that $a < b$ if and only if $a^c < b^c$. [*Hint:* Prove first that $a < b$ implies $a^c < b^c$; then use trichotomy to prove that $a^c < b^c$ implies $a < b$.]

4. Show that when $a < b$ then $a < b + c$.

5. If $a \neq 1$, prove the existence of b such that $a = b + 1$.

6. Prove (b) of Lemma 4.

7. (a) Show that each of $((a + b) + c) + d$, $(a + b) + (c + d)$, $a + (b + (c + d))$, $(a + (b + c)) + d$, $a + ((b + c) + d)$ is equal to the first.

(b) In view of (a), can you give a justification for the use of the symbol $a + b + c + d$?

(c) Find the "legal" parenthesizings of $a + b + c + d + e$, and show that each of them yields the same result.

(d) Formulate the general associative law.

(e) Prove the law given in (d).

8. Let $S_1(n)$ be the sum of the first n natural numbers.

(a) Compute $2S_1(n)$ for $n = 1, 2, 3, 7, 10, 14$.

(b) Guess a general formula for $2S_1(n)$.

(c) Prove the formula given in (b).

9. Let $S_1(n)$ be as in the preceding problem and define $S_3(n)$ to be the sum of the cubes of the first n natural numbers. Prove $S_3(n) = (S_1(_q))^2$. [*Hint:* You may use the result of the preceding problem.]

10. Find and prove a formula for

$$a + (a + d) + (a + 2d) + \cdots + (a + nd).$$

11. Prove $1 + na < (1 + a)^n$ for $1 < n$.

12. Given a, b show that there is a smallest c such that $a < bc$.

13. (a) Given $a < b$ show that there is a largest c such that $ac \leq b$.

(b) Repeat (a) with $\leq$ changed to $<$. [*Hint:* For (a), let $\bar{c}$ be the smallest natural number such that $b < a\bar{c}$. Show that $\bar{c} \neq 1$, and let $c + 1 = \bar{c}$. Now show that c is the desired number.]

14. Show that our axioms for the natural numbers are *not* "independent" by proving axiom (vii) from the earlier ones.

15. Prove that $3^n < n!$ for $n \geq 7$ ($n!$ is the product of all the natural numbers from 1 to n inclusive).

II.3. A Theorem in Arithmetic

In this section we touch upon that branch of mathematics known as the "theory of numbers." In the classical sense this phrase means "theory of integers." The first lemma is the "division algorithm" in the form required when we have only the natural numbers.

LEMMA 1.   *If $a < b$, then there are q and r such that $b = aq + r$, $r \leq a$.*

Proof: By exercise 13(b), p. 34, there is a largest number, we call it q here, such that $aq < b$. By axiom (vi)(a) there is an integer, we call it r here, such that $aq + r = b$. If $r > a$, then $aq + r > aq + a = a(q + 1) \geq b$, which is not the case. Hence, $r \leq a$, and the lemma is proved.

LEMMA 2.   *If $ab + c = ad$, then there is an f such that $c = af$.*

Proof: From $ab + c = ad$ we have $ab < ad$. Hence, by exercise 2(a), p. 33, $b < d$. Now there is a number, call it f, such that $b + f = d$. Multiplying by a yields $ab + af = ad$. But then $ab + c = ab + af$ and, by exercise 1(b), p. 33, $c = af$. This completes the proof.

Thus, Lemma 2 assures us that in an equation of the form $a + c = b$ every common factor of a and b must "divide" c. (A natural number a *divides* the natural number b it there is a natural number c such that $b = ac$. Both a and c are called *factors* of b.)

We now come to a somewhat deeper theorem to whose proof we are dedicating this section. We need first to define *prime number*. A prime number is a natural number other than 1 which has no natural number factors other than 1 and itself. The first nine prime numbers are $2, 3, 5, 7, 11, 13, 17, 19, 23$.

The theorem we are going to prove tells us that when a prime divides a product it must divide one of the factors in the product. For instance, 7 divides $3 \cdot 14$. Hence, 7 divides 3 or 7 divides 14. Clearly, 7 divides 14 in this case.

THEOREM.   *If p is a prime and p divides ab, then p divides a or p divides b. (Note that p may divide both a and b.)*

Proof: If p divides b, there is nothing to prove. Hence, we assume p does not divide b. Define S_b to be the set of all s such that p divides sb but p does not divide s. We hope to show that S_b is empty, since then a cannot be in S_b, and so p divides a. Suppose then that S_b is not empty. By axiom (viii) there is a smallest element $\bar{a}$ in S_b. There are now two cases, $\bar{a} < p$ and $\bar{a} > p$.

  (a) $\bar{a} < p$.

By Lemma 1 there are q and r such that

$$p = q\bar{a} + r, \qquad r \leq \bar{a}.$$

If $r = \bar{a}$, then $p = q\bar{a} + \bar{a} = (q + 1)\bar{a}$, and $\bar{a}$ divides p. Since p is a prime and $\bar{a} < p$ this implies $\bar{a} = 1$. But since $\bar{a}$ is in S_b this means that p divides $\bar{a}b = b$, which is not the case. Hence, $r < \bar{a}$. But now multiplying $p = q\bar{a} + r$ by b gives $pb = q\bar{a}b + rb$. By Lemma 2, since p divides $\bar{a}b$, we conclude that p divides rb. But this plus the fact that p does not divide r means r is in S_b. This contradicts the definition of $\bar{a}$ as being the smallest element of S_b.

  (b) $\bar{a} > p$.

By Lemma 1 above there are q and r such that

$$\bar{a} = qp + r, \qquad r \leq p < \bar{a}.$$

Multiplying $\bar{a} = qp + r$ by b gives $\bar{a}b = qbp + rb$. By Lemma 2 [as in case (a)] p divides rb, and we get the same contradiction as in case (a). This shows that the supposition that S_b was nonempty is false and completes the proof of the theorem.

  COROLLARY. *If p is a prime and p divides the product $a_1 \cdots a_n$, then p divides at least one of $a_1, \cdots, a_n$.*

  Proof: See exercise 6, p. 37.

● E X E R C I S E S

  1. Prove that q and r in Lemma 1, p. 35, are unique.

  2. Prove that if $a = d\bar{a}, b = d\bar{b}, a < b$, then there is an f such that $b = a + df$.

  3. Prove there is only one even prime.

  4. (a) Disprove the proposition: If p divides ab then p divides a or p divides b.

  (b) Does this contradict the theorem on p. 35? Explain.

  (c) Can you generalize the theorem on p. 35?

[*Hint:* For (c), what should we mean when we say that two integers are "relatively prime"? Now suppose m divides ab but is relatively prime to a.]?

5. (a) Let p, q, r be primes. Make a complete list of the divisors of pqr; pq^2r^3.

(b) How many divisors does

$$p_1^{\alpha_1} p_2^{\alpha_2} \cdots p_r^{\alpha_r}$$

have when $p_1, \cdots, p_r$ are distinct primes?

6. Prove the corollary to the theorem on p. 36.

7.* (a) Prove that every natural number greater than 1 can be written as the product of a finite number of prime numbers (each prime itself is regarded as a product of prime numbers).

(b) Prove that the factorization in (a) is unique.

[*Hint:* For (a), let S be the set of natural numbers greater than 1 for which the proposition is false, and apply the least integer principle. For (b), make use of the corollary to the theorem.]

8. Prove the following variant of Lemma 2. Let S be a collection of natural numbers such that:

(i) the number a is in S;

(ii) when all n satisfying $a \leq n \bigotimes b$ are in S, then b is in S. Then S contains all natural numbers $c \geq a$.

9. Repeat exercise 7(a) using exercise 8.

II.4. Subtraction in Z

Axiom (vi)(a) tells us that when $a < b$ there exists a unique c such that $a + c = b$. For example, $3 < 13$ and $3 + 10 = 13$. The $a, b,$ and c in this example are, respectively, 3, 13, and 10.

When $a < b$ we denote the unique c, such that $a + c = b$, by the symbol $b - a$. Thus, when $a, b,$ and c are respectively 3, 13, and 10 we have $13 - 3 = 10$.

The above discussion shows us how to introduce a new operation, denoted by $-$, into Z. This operation has as domain the set of ordered pairs (b, a), where $a < b$. This operation is not closed, since there are many pairs of elements of Z not in the domain of the operation. For instance, $(3, 13)$ is not in the domain. Thus, $3 - 13$ is not defined, whereas $13 - 3$ *is* defined.

We read "$b - a$" as "b minus a" and refer to the process of computing $b - a$ as "subtracting a from b." Thus, when we say "subtract 3 from 13" we mean "find the number c such that $3 + c = 13$."

The remainder of this section is devoted to a derivation of eight useful properties of the subtraction operation, which we shall number (1) through (8). In some of our derivations we shall write the number of previously obtained results over an equal sign which these previous results justify. Thus, we may write A $\overset{3}{=}$ B where we mean that applying property (3) to A will yield B. Where no such numeral is appended to the equality the expression will generally be true by virtue of commutativity or associativity of addition or multiplication.

(1) If $a < b$, then $a + (b - a) = b$.

Proof: This is immediate from the definition of $b - a$.

(2) If $a < b$, then $a = b - (b - a)$.

Proof: This follows from $(b - a) + a = b$.

(3) $a = (a + b) - b$.

Proof: Since $b + a = a + b$, this follows from the definition of $(a + b) - b$.

(4) If $a < b$, then $c + (b - a) = (c + b) - a$.

Proof: $c + (b - a) \overset{3}{=} \{[c + (b - a)] + a\} - a = \{c + [(b - a) + a]\} - a \overset{1}{=} (c + b) - a$.

(5) If $a + b < c$, then $(c - a) - b = c - (a + b)$.

Proof: $a < c$ and $b < c - a$. Now $(c - a) - b \overset{3}{=} \{[(c - a) - b] + (a + b)\} - (a + b) = \{[(c - a) - b] + (b + a)\} - (a + b) = (\{[(c - a) - b] + b\} + a) - (a + b) \overset{1}{=} [(c - a) + a] - (a + b) \overset{1}{=} c - (a + b)$.

(6) If $a < b$, then $(b + c) - (a + c) = b - a$, and $b + c = (a + c) + (b - a)$.

Proof: $(b + c) - (a + c) = (b + c) - (c + a) \overset{5}{=} [(b + c) - c] - a \overset{3}{=} b - a$. The second half follows from the first half by adding $a + c$ to both sides.

(7) If $a < b$, then $c(b - a) = cb - ca$.

Proof: From (1), $ca + c(b - a) = cb$, and the result follows.

(8) If $a < b$ and $c < d$, then $(b - a)(d - c) = (bd + ac) - (ad + bc)$.

Proof: $(b - a)(d - c) \overset{7}{=} (b - a)d - (b - a)c = (bd - ad) - (bc - ac) \overset{5}{=} bd - [ad + (bc - ac)] \overset{4}{=} bd - [(ad + bc) - ac] \overset{3}{=} [(bd + ac) - ac] - [(ad + bc) - ac] \overset{5}{=} (bd + ac) - \{ac + [(ad + bc) - ac]\} \overset{1}{=} (bd + ac) - (ad + bc)$.

● EXERCISES

1. Show that if $a + x = b$ has a solution, then
   (a) the solution in unique;
   (b) $a < b$.
[*Hint:* For (a), you might use exercise 1(b), p. 33.]

2. If $c < a$ and $c < b$, then $a + (b - c) = b + (a - c)$.

3. Disprove: $a - (b - c) = (a - b) + c$. Can you find some conditions which make this a true equality?

4.* Show that when $a < b$ then $(b - a)^2 = (a^2 + b^2) - (2ab)$.

5.* (a) Let $(S; \Theta; R)$ be an algebraic system in which Θ is closed, commutative, and associative and in which R is a linear order relation. Further, suppose that the equation

$$s\Theta x = s', \; (s \text{ and } s' \text{ are in } S)$$

has a solution for x in S if and only if sRs'. Let D be the subset of $S \times S$ consisting precisely of the pairs (s, s'), where sRs'. Define a new operation $\bar{\Theta}$ in S, with domain D, as follows:

$$s'\bar{\Theta}s \text{ is the solution of } s\Theta x = s'.$$

Prove: (1) If sRs', then $s\Theta(s'\bar{\Theta}s) = s'$.
   (2) If sRs', then $s = s'\bar{\Theta}(s'\bar{\Theta}s)$.
   (3) $s = (s\Theta s')\bar{\Theta}s'$.
   (4) If sRs', then $s''\Theta(s'\bar{\Theta}s) = (s''\Theta s')\bar{\Theta}s$.
   (5) If $(s\Theta s')Rs''$, then $(s''\bar{\Theta}s)\bar{\Theta}s' = s''\bar{\Theta}(s\Theta s')$.
   (6) If sRs', then
      (i) $(s'\Theta s'')\bar{\Theta}(s\Theta s'') = s''\bar{\Theta}s$;
      (ii) $s'\Theta s'' = (s\Theta s'')\Theta(s'\bar{\Theta}s)$,

(b) Let $(S; \Theta, \Theta'; R)$ be the system in part (a) with the additional operation Θ' which is closed and distributive over Θ.

Prove: (7) If sRs', then $s''\Theta'(s'\bar{\Theta}s) = (s''\Theta's')\bar{\Theta}(s''\Theta's)$,

       (8) If sRs' and $s''Rs'''$, then

$$(s'\bar{\Theta}s)\Theta'(s'''\bar{\Theta}s'') = [(s'\Theta's''')\Theta(s\Theta's'')]\bar{\Theta}[(s\Theta's''')\Theta(s'\Theta's'')].$$

(c) Show that the contents of Section II.4 are contained in the systems in (a) and (b).

(d) For the system in (b), prove:

      (9) $sR(s\Theta s')$.

    (10) If sRs', then $(s\Theta s'')R(s'\Theta s'')$.

    (11) If sRs', then $(s\Theta's'')R(s'\Theta's'')$.

[*Hint for part* (d): For (10) and (11) see exercise 14, p. 34.]

III The Positive Rational Numbers

$Z : N = P$
$R = R^+$
I^* is non 0 Integers

III.1. The Need for an Extension

Consider the equation $ax = b$, where a and b are in Z, and ask the question, "Does $ax = b$ have a solution in Z; that is, is there a natural number x such that $ax = b$?" The answer might well be, "It depends on the values of a and b." For, if $a = 2$, $b = 6$, there is such a natural number x, namely $x = 3$; whereas if $a = 6$, $b = 2$, there is no such natural number.

Since $ax = b$ has no solution for some elements a, b in Z, we seek an extension $(R; \oplus, \odot; \oslash)$ of $(Z; +, \cdot; <)$ in which every equation of the form $a \odot x = b$, for a, b in R, has a solution. Recall from Section I.8 that $(R; \oplus, \odot; \oslash)$ is an *extension* of $(Z; +, \cdot; <)$ if there exists a subset, say Z_R, of R such that $(Z_R; \oplus, \odot; \oslash) \cong (Z; +, \cdot, <)$. Furthermore, we shall want the extension $(R; \oplus, \odot; \oslash)$ to be such that:

(i) it is closed with respect to $\oplus$ and $\odot$;

(ii) it is linearly ordered with respect to $\oslash$;

(iii) $\oplus$ and $\odot$ are commutative;

(vi) $\oplus$ and $\odot$ are associative;

(v) $\odot$ is distributive over $\oplus$.

We shall proceed to the construction of a set R and define two operations $\oplus$ and $\odot$ in R and a relation $\oslash$ in R such that the system $(R; \oplus, \odot; \oslash)$ has all of the desired properties. In order to construct the set R, we introduce the notion of two elements of $Z \times Z$ being "equivalent."

If (a, b) and (c, d) in $Z \times Z$ are such that $ad = bc$, then we call (a, b) and (c, d) *equivalent*, and we write $(a, b) \sim (c, d)$.

In our next lemma we state three properties of this relation.

41

LEMMA 1.

(i) $(a, b) \sim (a, b)$;

(ii) $(a, b) \sim (c, d)$ *if and only if* $(c, d) \sim (a, b)$;

(iii) $(a, b) \sim (c, d)$ *and* $(c, d) \sim (e, f)$ *implies* $(a, b) \sim (e, f)$.

Proof: See exercise 1, below.

The set of all elements of $Z \times Z$ which are equivalent to a given fixed element of $Z \times Z$ is called an *equivalence class* of $Z \times Z$. If the fixed element is $(1, 1)$, the equivalence class of all elements equivalent to $(1, 1)$ is

$$\{(1, 1), (2, 2), (3, 3), (4, 4), \cdots\}.$$

Similarly, for the fixed elements $(3, 6)$, $(4, 2)$, $(52, 68)$, and $(31, 3)$ the equivalence classes are

$$\{(1, 2), (2, 4), (3, 6), (4, 8), (5, 10), (6, 12), \cdots\},$$
$$\{(2, 1), (4, 2), (6, 3), (8, 4), (10, 5), (12, 6), \cdots\},$$
$$\{(13, 17), (26, 34), (39, 51), (52, 68), (65, 85), \cdots\},$$
$$\{(31, 3), (62, 6), (93, 9), (124, 12), (155, 15), \cdots\}.$$

LEMMA 2.   *If* S_1 *and* S_2 *are equivalence classes of* $Z \times Z$, *then either* S_1 *and* S_2 *are identical or they are disjoint (have no elements in common).*

Proof: See exercise 2, below.

We now define R to be the collection of all equivalence classes of $Z \times Z$. Thus, the *elements* in R are *equivalence classes* of $Z \times Z$. For example, the equivalence class

$$\{(13, 17), (26, 34), (39, 51), (52, 68), (65, 85), \cdots\},$$

given above, is a single element in R.

● EXERCISES

1. Prove Lemma 1, above.

2. Prove Lemma 2, above.

3. Let S be an equivalence class of $Z \times Z$. Prove:

(i) if (a, b) and (c, d) are in S, than $(a, b) \sim (c, d)$;

(ii) if (a, b) is in S and $(c, d) \sim (a, b)$, then (c, d) is in S.

[*Hint:* Let S_1 be the equivalence class of elements equivalent to (a, b), and let S_2 be the equivalence class of elements equivalent to (c, d). Use Lemma 1 to show that every element in S_1 is equivalent to (c, d) *if* there is an element (e, f) in both S_1 and S_2. This shows that every element in S_1 is in S_2. Repeat to show that every element in S_2 is in S_1, and conclude that $S_1 = S_2$.]

4. Show that the set $\{(3, 1), (9, 3), (12, 4), (15, 5), (18, 6), \cdots\}$ is not an equivalence class of $Z \times Z$. Is this class a subset of any equivalence class of $Z \times Z$? Repeat with the set $\{(17, 2), (34, 4), (50, 6), (68, 8), \cdots\}$.

5. Let M be an arbitrary natural number and S be an equivalence class of $Z \times Z$. Show there exists in S an element (a, b) for which both a and b exceed M. Taking M = 1000, exhibit such elements for each of the five sample equivalence classes displayed in the text.

6. Prove that every element of $Z \times Z$ is in some element of R.

7. Prove that the following prescription for an "operation" ∗ in R does not "really define" an operation in R.

Let r and r' be in R, and let (a, b) be in r and (c, d) be in r'. Put $r∗r' = r''$, where r'' is that equivalence class containing $(a + c, b + d)$.

[*Hint:* By working with examples show that it is quite possible for two people to start with the same classes r and r' and obtain via this "definition" different classes r''. Explain why this is intolerable.]

III.2. Definition of ⊙ in R

The definitions we are going to make for our operations in R will proceed along the lines of the "definition" given in exercise 7, above. We must, of course, make sure that they do not fail to be definitions as did that one. Whenever we define an operation in a collection of sets by making use of particular elements of the sets we must be sure that the choice of these elements is really immaterial—that any choice would lead to the same result. In exercise 7, above, we found that the choice of (a, b) in r and (c, d) in r' definitely influenced the resulting r''. Our next lemma is to assure us that a similar situation is not going to be true for the definition of $\odot$ that we adopt in this section.

LEMMA.   *Let r and r' be elements of* R. *Further, let (a, b), (c, d) be in r and (a', b'), (c', d') be in r'. Then $(aa', bb') \sim (cc', dd')$.*

Proof: We need to show that $aa'dd' = bb'cc'$. By exercise 3, p. 42, $(a, b) \sim (c, d)$ and $(a', b') \sim (c', d')$.   Therefore, $ad = bc$ and $a'd' = b'c'$. Multiplying these equations together gives the desired result.

This lemma gives us the important fact that if r and r' are two elements of R, then there is a third element r'' of R such that whenever (a, b) is in r and (c, d) is in r' then (ac, bd) is in r''. That there is only one such r'' is a consequence of Lemma 2, p. 42. We can therefore make the following definition.

DEFINITION. $r \odot r'$ *is that r'' such that (ac, bd) is in r'' whenever (a, b) is in r and (c, d) is in r'.*

We sometimes make this sort of definition with no lemma preceding it and then ask if the operation ($\odot$ in this case) is "well-defined." An affirmative answer is then forthcoming by a proof of a lemma such as that above.

This definition assures us that $\odot$ is closed.

Note that we do not define $r = r'$ to be that subset of $Z \times Z$ containing all (ac, bd) with (a, b) in r and (c, d) in r'. This collection would not necessarily be an element of R. For instance, consider the two elements r and r' in R, where $r = \{(1, 2), (2, 4), (3, 6), (4, 8), \cdots\}$ and $r' = \{(2, 1), (4, 2), (6, 3), (8, 4), \cdots\}$. Then the set of all (ac, bd) for (a, b) in r and (c, d) in r' is $\{(2, 2), (4, 4), (6, 6), (8, 8), \cdots\}$, which is not an element of R. However, this set is a subset of the set $\{(1, 1), (2, 2), (3, 3), \cdots\}$, which *is* an element of R. The product $r \odot r'$ is $\{(1, 1), (2, 2), (3, 3), \cdots\}$.

The next two lemmas prove that $\odot$ is commutative and associative.

LEMMA. $r \odot r' = r' \odot r$ *for all r, r' in* R.

Proof: Let (a, b) be in r and (c, d) be in r'. Then $r \odot r'$ is that r'' in R containing (ac, bd), and $r' \odot r$ is that r'' in R containing (ca, db).

But since $ac = ca$, $bd = db$, we have $(ac, bd) = (ca, db)$, and therefore by Lemma 2, p. 42, $r\odot r' = r'\odot r$.

LEMMA. $r\odot(r'\odot r'') = (r\odot r')\odot r''$ for all r, r', r'' in R.

Proof: Let (a, b), (c, d), (e, f) be in r, r', r'' respectively. Then $(a(ce), b(df))$ is in $r\odot(r'\odot r'')$, and $((ac)e, (bd)f)$ is in $(r\odot r')\odot r''$. But since $a(ce) = (ac)e$ and $b(df) = (bd)f$, we have $(a(ce), b(df)) = ((ac)e, (bd)f)$ and so, by Lemma 2, p. 42, $r\odot(r'\odot r'') = (r\odot r')\odot r''$.

We now define a special subset of R. We denote the subset by Z_R.

DEFINITION. Z_R *contains r of R if and only if r contains an element of the form $(a, 1)$.*

From this definition we see that the elements

$$\{(5, 1), (10, 2), (15, 3), \cdots\},$$
$$\{(102, 1), (204, 2), (306, 3), \cdots\}$$

of R are elements of Z_R while the elements

$$\{(7, 2), (14, 4), (21, 6), \cdots\},$$
$$\{(36, 11), (72, 22), (108, 33), \cdots\}$$

of R and not elements of Z_R.

Note that for each natural number n in Z there is exactly one element of Z_R containing $(n, 1)$, namely, $\{(n, 1), (2n, 2), (3n, 3), (4n, 4), \cdots\}$.

The next lemma proves that Z_R with its operation $\odot$ is "essentially the same" as Z with the operation of ordinary multiplication.

LEMMA. $(Z; \cdot) \cong (Z_R; \odot)$.

Proof: If f is the mapping which takes n in Z into that element of Z_R containing $(n, 1)$, then f is a 1 to 1 mapping of Z onto Z_R. Denote the element of Z_R which contains $(n, 1)$ by $\overline{(n, 1)}$. We need to show that $f(n \cdot m) = f(n)\odot f(m)$ for all n, m in Z. But $f(n \cdot m) = \overline{(nm, 1)}$, while $f(n) = \overline{(n, 1)}$, $f(m) = \overline{(m, 1)}$. Hence, since $(nm, 1)$ is in $\overline{(n, 1)}\odot\overline{(m, 1)}$, we must have $\overline{(nm, 1)} = \overline{(n, 1)}\odot\overline{(m, 1)}$. This completes the proof.

COROLLARY. $(R; \odot)$ *is an extension of* $(Z; \cdot)$.

● EXERCISES

1. Prove the remark that to each n in Z there is exactly one element of Z_R containing $(n, 1)$.

2.* Prove that if r is in R, then:

(i) (a, b) is in r implies that (ka, kb) is in r for k any positive integer;

(ii) (ka, kb) is in r for k, a, b in Z implies that (a, b) is in r.

3.* Prove that each r in R contains exactly one ordered pair (a, b), where a and b have no common factor other than 1. Prove also, for this a and b, that if $(c, d) \sim (a, b)$, then there is a k such that $c = ka, d = kb$.
[*Hint:* By exercise 7(a), p. 37, and the corollary on p. 36 the existence of at least one such pair (a, b) is guaranteed. Suppose then that (a, b) and (c, d) were two such pairs in the same r of R. Then $ad = bc$, and again using exercise 7, p. 37, deduce that $a = c, b = d$.]

4. Prove in $(R; \odot)$ that $(r \odot r') \odot (r'' \odot r''') = r' \odot (r'' \odot (r \odot r'''))$.

5.* Find the $\odot$-identity in $(R; \odot)$.

6.* Let $\acute{e}$ designate the $\odot$-identity of $(R; \odot)$. Show that the equation $r \odot x = \acute{e}$ always has a solution in $(R; \odot)$. [*Hint:* Choose an arbitrary element, say (a, b), in r and take x to be that element of R containing (b, a) as an element.]

7.* Prove that in $(R; \odot)$ the equation $r \odot x = r'$ has a unique solution. [*Hint:* If $\bar{r}$ designates a solution of the equation $r \odot x = \acute{e}$, then the equation $r \odot x = r'$ has the unique solution $x = \bar{r} \odot r'$.] (Note that this tells us that the particular equation $r \odot x = \acute{e}$ has a unique solution.)

8. Give some sort of motivation for the notion of equivalence we gave for elements of $Z \times Z$ and for the definition of $\odot$ in R. [*Hint:* Suppose we write the ordered pair (a, b) as a/b.]

9. Let $S = Z \times Z$ and define the operation $*$ in S as follows: If $(a, b), (c, d)$ are in S, then $(a, b) * (c, d) = (ac + bd, bc + ad)$. Show that $(S; *)$ is closed with respect to $*$ and that $*$ is commutative and associative. Is there any problem about whether $*$ is really defined? Explain.

10. Prove that the following prescription for an "operation"* in R does not really define an operation. Let r, r' be in R and (a, b), (c, d) be in r, r', respectively. Put $r*r' = r''$ where r'' is that class containing $(a + c, bd)$.

III.3. Definition of $\oplus$ in R

Exercises 5–7, p. 46, show us that $(R; \odot)$ is an extension of $(Z; \cdot)$ in which the equation $r \odot x = r'$ is always uniquely solvable. However, we are not finished with our present program, since we want an extension $(R; \oplus, \odot; \oslash)$ of $(Z; +, \cdot; <)$ [not just $(R; \odot)$ of $(Z; \cdot)$] in which $r \odot x = r'$ is always solvable. Therefore, our next job is to introduce a new operation $\oplus$ into $(R; \odot)$.

As in Section III.2, it is again necessary to prove a preliminary lemma.

LEMMA. *Let r and r' be elements of* R. *Further, let (a, b), (c, d) be in r and (a', b'), (c', d') be in r'. Then $(ab' + ba', bb')$ $\sim (cd' + dc', dd')$.*

Proof: We need to show that $(ab' + ba')dd' = bb'(cd' + dc')$. By exercise 3, p. 42, $(a, b) \sim (c, d)$ and $(a', b') \sim (c', d')$. Therefore, $ad = bc$ and $a'd' = b'c'$. Multiplying the equation $ad = bc$ on both sides by $b'd'$ and the equation $a'd' = b'c'$ on both sides by bd gives the equations

$$ab'dd' = bb'cd'$$
$$a'bdd' = bb'c'd.$$

Adding these equations gives the desired result.

This lemma tells us that if r and r' are two elements of R, then there is a third element r'' of R such that whenever (a, b) is in r and (c, d) is in r' then $(ad + bc, bd)$ is in r''. That there is only one such r'' is a consequence of Lemma 2, p. 42. We therefore make the following definition.

DEFINITION. $r \oplus r'$ *is that r'' such that $(ad + bc, bd)$ is in r'' whenever (a, b) is in r and (c, d) is in r'.*

This definition assures us that $\oplus$ is closed.

Note that we do not define $r \oplus r'$ to be that subset of $Z \times Z$

containing all $(ad + bc, bd)$ with (a, b) in r and (c, d) in r'. For instance, if r is in R and $r = r' = \{(1, 2), (2, 4), (3, 6), (4, 8), \cdots\}$, then the set of all $(ad + bc, bd)$, for (a, b), (c, d) in r, is $\{(4, 4), (8, 8), (12, 12), (16, 16), \cdots\}$, which is not an element of R. However, this set is a subset of the set $\{(1, 1), (2, 2), (3, 3), (4, 4), \cdots\}$, which *is* an element of R. The sum $r \oplus r'$ is $\{(1, 1), (2, 2), (3, 3), (4, 4), \cdots\}$.

The next two lemmas prove that $\oplus$ is commutative and associative.

LEMMA. $r \oplus r' = r' \oplus r$ *for all* r, r' *in* R.

Proof: Let (a, b) be in r and (c, d) be in r'. Then $r \oplus r'$ is that r in R containing $(ad + bc, bd)$, and $r' + r$ is that r in R containing $(cb + da, db)$. But since $ad = da$, $bc = cb$, $bd = db$, we have $(ad + bc, bd) = (cb + da, db)$, and therefore by Lemma 2, p. 42, $r \oplus r' = r' \oplus r$.

LEMMA. $r \oplus (r' \oplus r'') = (r \oplus r') \oplus r''$ *for all* r, r', r'' *in* R.

Proof: Let (a, b), (c, d), (e, f) be in r, r', r'', respectively. Then $(a(df) + b(cf + de), b(df))$ is in $r \oplus (r' \oplus r'')$, and $((ad + bc)f + (bd)e, (bd)f)$ is in $(r \oplus r') \oplus r''$. But since $a(df) + b(cf + de) = (ad + bc)f + (bd)e$ and $b(df) = (bd)f$, we have $(a(df) + b(cf + de), b(df)) = ((ad + bc)f + (bd)e, (bd)f)$ and therefore by Lemma 2, p. 42, $r \oplus (r' \oplus r'') = (r \oplus r') \oplus r''$.

We show next that $\odot$ is distributive over $\oplus$.

LEMMA. $r \odot (r' \oplus r'') = (r \odot r') \oplus (r \odot r'')$ *for all* r, r', r'' *in* R.

Proof: Let (a, b), (c, d), (e, f) be in r, r', r'', respectively. Then $(a(cf + de), b(df))$ is in $r \odot (r' \oplus r'')$ and $((ac)(bf) + (bd)(ae), (bd)(bf))$ is in $(r \odot r') \oplus (r \odot r'')$. Now $((ac)(bf) + (bd)(ae), (bd)(bf)) = (acbf + bdae, bdbf) \sim (acf + dae, dbf) = (a(cf + de), b(df))$. Hence, the equivalence class $r \odot (r' \oplus r'')$ has an element in common with the equivalence class $(r \odot r') \oplus (r \odot r'')$. The conclusion now follows from Lemma 2, p. 42.

● EXERCISES

1. Is there a $\oplus$-identity in $(R; \oplus, \odot)$?

2. Prove in $(R; \oplus, \odot)$ that $r\oplus(r'\oplus(r''\oplus(r'''))) = r'\oplus(r'' \oplus(r\oplus r'''))$.

3.* Let Z_R be as defined on p. 45. Defining $\oplus$, $\odot$ in Z_R as they were defined in R prove $(Z; +, \cdot) \cong (Z_R; \oplus, \odot)$. [*Hint:* In virtue of the last lemma in Section III.2, you need only show that the mapping f given there has the additional property $f(n + m) = f(n)\oplus f(m)$.]

4. Let $\overline{(a, b)}$ be that element of R containing (a, b) where a, b are elements of Z. Solve in $(R; \oplus, \odot)$:
   (a) $\overline{(3, 4)}\oplus r = \overline{(7, 8)}$;
   (b) $\overline{(3, 4)}\odot r = \overline{(7, 8)}$;
   (c) $(\overline{(3, 4)}\odot r)\oplus\overline{(2, 1)} = \overline{(7, 3)}$.

5. Let $S = Z \times Z$ and define the operation $**$ in S as follows. If (a, b), (c, d) are in S, then $(a, b)**(c, d) = (a + c, b + d)$. Show that $(S; **)$ is closed with respect to $**$ and that $**$ is commutative and associative. Is there any problem about whether $**$ is really defined? Explain.

6. Consider the system $(S; **, *)$, where S and $**$ are as defined in exercise 4 above and $*$ is as defined in exercise 9, p. 46. Is $*$ distributive over $**$? Prove your answer.

III.4. Definition of $\bigodot$ in R

As in Section III.2 and III.3, again a preliminary lemma is needed before our definition can be given.

LEMMA. *Let r and r' be elements of* R. *Further, let (a, b), (c, d) be in r and (a', b'), (c', d') be in r'. Then $ab' < a'b$ implies $cd' < c'd$.*

Proof: $(a, b) \sim (c, d)$ and $(a', b') \sim (c', d')$, so $bc = ad$ and $a'd' = b'c'$. Multiplying these equations gives $bca'd' = adb'c'$. Multiplying $ab' < a'b$ by dc' gives $ab'dc' < a'bdc'$. This with the above equality gives $bca'd' < a'bdc'$. Cancelling $a'b$ yields $cd' < c'd$, the desired result.

This lemma tells us that if some element (a, b) in r has the property that $ab' < a'b$ for some element (a', b') in r', then every element (c, d) in r bears this relationship to every element (c', d') in r'; that is, $cd' < c'd$ for all (c, d) in r and (c', d') in r'.

We therefore make the following definition.

DEFINITION. $\ominus$ *is the set of all* (r, r'), r, r' *in* R, *such that* $ab' < a'b$ *whenever* (a, b) *is in* r *and* (a', b') *is in* r'.

We will, as usual, write $r \ominus r'$ when (r, r') is in $\ominus$. Thus, $r \ominus r'$ if and only if for (a, b) in r and (a', b') in r' it is true that $ab' < a'b$.

● EXERCISES

1. Can $r \ominus r'$ and $r' \ominus r$ both be true for r, r' in R? Prove your answer.

2.* Prove that the system $(\mathrm{R}; \oplus, \odot; \ominus)$ is linearly ordered with respect to $\ominus$.

3.* Prove that the equation

$$r \oplus x = r'$$

is solvable in R if and only if $r \ominus r'$.

4.* Prove that when $r \oplus x = r'$ is solvable the solution is unique.

5.* Prove the following:

$$(\mathrm{Z}; +, \cdot\, ; <) \cong (\mathrm{Z_R}; \oplus, \odot; \ominus).$$

III.5. Final Remarks for Chapter III

Putting together the results of Sections III.2, III.3, and III.4 we know the following for the system $(\mathrm{R}; \oplus, \odot; \ominus)$:

(a) It satisfies properties (i)–(v) on p. 41.

(b) Every equation of the form $r \odot x = r'$ has a unique solution in R.

(c) There exists a subset $\mathrm{Z_R}$ of R such that $(\mathrm{Z_R}; \oplus, \odot; \ominus) \cong (\mathrm{Z}; +, \cdot\, ; <)$.

Hence, we have carried out that part of our program set out in Section III.1.

The system $(\mathrm{R}; \oplus, \odot; \ominus)$ will be called the collection of *positive rational* numbers. The elements of $\mathrm{Z_R}$ will be called the *positive integers*. (Note that the word "positive" here has, as yet, no independent meaning.)

From now on we work with elements of the set $(R; \oplus, \odot; \oslash)$ only. We shall not use the collection Z of natural numbers again. (When we need a natural number we may use the corresponding rational number instead.) Hence there will be no ambiguity if, for convenience, we use the symbol 3 for that element of R containing $(3, 1)$, 5 for that element of R containing $(5, 1)$, and so on, and n for that element of R containing $(n, 1)$. Then $3 \oplus 5 = 8$, $3 \odot 5 = 15$, $3 \oslash 5$, $8 \oslash 15$, and so on, as we know from our knowledge of $(R; \oplus, \odot; \oslash)$. Since we are not going to use Z, we will not need the symbols $+$, $\cdot$, $<$ as used in connection with Z. Hence, we take them over and use them in R instead of the more cumbersome $\oplus$, $\odot$, $\oslash$. Hence, the system $(R; \oplus, \odot; \oslash)$ will be written $(R; +, \cdot ; <)$. Then the phrase $3 + 4 < 8$ means that if r, r', r'' are the elements of R containing $(3, 1)$, $(4, 1)$, $(8, 1)$, respectively, then $r \oplus r' \oslash r''$. Those elements of R not in Z_R will be written as before. Hence $r + r' < r''$ means $r \oplus r' \oslash r''$.

Furthermore, if (a, b) is in r, r in R, we shall designate r by a/b. Note that this gives rise to many designations for each element r of R. For example $(1, 2)$, $(2, 4)$, $(3, 6)$, $(4, 8)$, $\cdots$ are all in $r = \{(1, 2), (2, 4), (3, 6), (4, 8), \cdots\}$, which is an element of R. Hence, $1/2, 2/4, 3/6, 4/8, \cdots$ are all designations for r. Since each of these designates the same element of R, we write $1/2 = 2/4 = 3/6 = 4/8 = \cdots$. Indeed, we manipulate these designations as if they were the numbers themselves, and we shall multiply and add them freely. Since $a/b = c/d$ if and only if (a, b) and (c, d) are equivalent, we have $a/b = c/d$ if and only if $ad = bc$. We use the expression $a/b + c/d$ as another way of writing $r + r'$, where (a, b) is in r and (c, d) is in r'. But $r + r' = r''$, where r'' contains $(ad + bc, bd)$. Hence, $a/b + c/d = r + r' = r'' = (ad + bc)/bd$. Similarly, $(a/b)(c/d) = ac/bd$. (See exercise 1, p. 52.)

By exercise 3, p. 46, each r in R contains exactly one pair (a, b) where a and b have no common factors greater than 1. Further, each such pair (a, b) is in some r of R. Hence, by our conventions above we shall speak of R as if it were the totality of a/b, where a and b have no common factors greater than 1, and these expressions are manipulated in accordance with the above remarks and the exercises on pp. 52–54.

The elements of Z_R are those elements in R which are designated by $1/1, 2/1, 3/1, 4/1, \cdots$. Since we shall be working in the system $(R; +, \cdot\ ; <)$, we shall, as mentioned above, replace $1/1, 2/1, 3/1, \cdots$ by the names of their images in Z (that is, replace the designation $n/1$ by n for all $n \geq 1$). Finally, we adopt the name Z for Z_R.

Having made these conventions, the results of this chapter show that every algebraic equation which can be solved in $(Z; +, \cdot\ ; <)$ can also be solved in $(R; +, \cdot\ ; <)$, but that there are algebraic equations which can be solved in $(R; +, \cdot\ ; <)$ which cannot be solved in $(Z; +, \cdot\ ; <)$. Because of this, we can legitimately claim that $(R; +, \cdot\ ; <)$ is "algebraically larger" than $(Z; +, \cdot\ ; <)$.

At first glance one might think that this means that $(R; +, \cdot\ ; <)$ has "more elements" than does $(Z; +, \cdot\ ; <)$. Indeed, to the beginner this may seem indisputable. In the appendix to this chapter we give a brief introduction to the theory of cardinal numbers in which we show, among other things, that the above two systems actually have "the same number of elements." This appendix is not necessary for an understanding of Chapters IV, V, and VI. The material is, however, a prerequisite for the additional discussion of cardinal numbers contained in Appendix A.

● EXERCISES

1.* Show that $(a/b)(c/d) = ac/bd$.

2.* Show that 1 is the $\cdot$-identity in $(R; +, \cdot\ ; <)$.

3.* Prove that the equation $(a/b)x = 1$ has a unique solution in R. Find the solution. This unique solution is called the $\cdot$ -*inverse* of a/b or the *reciprocal* of a/b.

4.* Prove that the equation $(a/b)x = c/d$ has a unique solution in R. Find the solution. Denote the unique solution of this equation by $(c/d) \div (a/b)$ or $(c/d) \oslash (a/b)$.

5.* By exercises 3 and 4, p. 50, we know $r + x = r'$ has a unique solution in R when $r < r'$. Give conditions on a, b, c, d such that $(a/b) + x = c/d$ has a unique solution in R, and when these conditions are satisfied give the solution. When $(a/b) + x = c/d$ has a solution we designate it by $(c/d) - (a/b)$.

6. Solve the following equations in R.

(i) $(5/4)x = 1$.

(ii) $(7/15)x = 33$.

(iii) $4x = 1/2$.

(iv) $x + (5/6) = 2/3$.

(v) $2x + (5/6) = 6/7$.

(vi) $(3/11)x + 31 = 13/15$.

(vii) $(47/39)x + (81/3) = 243/6$.

7.* From the above we have the following rules. When a, b, c, d are natural numbers,

(i) $(a/b) + (c/d) = (ad + bc)/bd$;

(ii) $(a/b)(c/d) = ac/bd$;

(iii) $(a/b) < (c/d)$ when $ad < bc$;

(iv) $(a/b) - (c/d) = (ad - bc)/bd$ when $(c/d) < (a/b)$;

(v) $(a/b) \div (c/d) = ad/bc$.

Prove (i) through (v) when a, b, c, d are replaced by arbitrary *elements of* R. Here, r/r' is to be interpreted to be $r \oslash r'$ as defined in exercise 4 above. In the sequel we shall frequently use rules (i) through (v), where a, b, c, d are arbitrary rational numbers.

8.* Show that given the fractions a/b, c/d there is an element q in Z such that $qa/b > c/d$ (Archimedean property). [*Hint:* Use the corresponding result for Z.]

9.* If r, r', r'' are in R and $r < r'$, prove:

(i) $rr'' < r'r''$;

(ii) $r + r'' < r' + r''$;

(iii) $r/r'' < r'/r''$;

(iv) $1/r' < 1/r$;

(v) $r < r + r''$;

(vi) $r/r' < 1$;

(vii) $\sqrt{r} < \sqrt{r'}$ (if both square roots exist);

(viii) $r^2 < r'^2$.

10.* Let a, b, c, m be arbitrary numbers in Z. Then if $n > max(b, (a + 1)m/c)$, prove that $(an + b)/cn^2 < 1/m$.

11. Show that when $a_1, a_2, a_3, a_4, a_5, a_6, a_7, m$ are in Z then for all "sufficiently large" n in Z we have $(a_1n^2 + a_2n + a_3)/(a_4n^3 + a_5n^2 + a_6n + a_7) < 1/m$. (First make precise the phrase "sufficiently large.")

12.* Prove $1 + nr < (1 + r)^n$ for $n > 1$, where r is in R, n in Z. [*Hint:* See exercise 11, p. 34.]

13.* Let m be in Z and a be in R, with $1 < a$. Show that there exists an n in Z such that $1/a^n < 1/m$. [*Hint:* Write $a = 1 + r$ with r in R and use exercises 8, 9, 12 above.]

14* (a) Show that in exercise 13, $1/a^n < 1/m$ for *all* "sufficiently large" n in Z.

(b) Show that for any fixed b in Z, $b/a^n < 1/m$ for all sufficiently large n.

15.* Rewrite Section II.4 in such a way that your version might properly be entitled "Subtraction in R." In particular, note that all of the properties (1) through (8), and those given in Exercises p. 39, have exact analogues. [*Hint:* Note that the reference to axiom (vi) (a) made on p. 37 will be replaced in your writeup by a reference to exercise 5, p. 52. See also exercise 5, p. 39.]

16.* Let Q_n designate the sum of 1 and the first n powers of q, where q is in R. That is, $Q_n = 1 + q + q^2 + \cdots + q^n$. Prove:

$$Q_n = \begin{cases} (q^{n+1} - 1)/(q - 1) \text{ when } 1 < q; \\ (1 - q^{n+1})/(1 - q) \text{ when } q < 1. \end{cases}$$

[*Hint:* For $1 < q$. In this case $qQ_n > Q_n$, so $qQ_n - Q_n$ is defined and is equal to $(q + \cdots + q^{n+1}) - (1 + q + \cdots + q^n)$. Write this last as $(q^{n+1} + (q + \cdots + q^n)) - (1 + (q + \cdots + q^n))$ and use the rational analogue of property (6) of Section II.4.]

Cardinal Numbers

1. Equivalence of Sets

We begin our discussion with an example. Suppose we ask if there are the same number of trees in the yard as there are people in the room. One way of determining the answer to the question is to count both the number of trees and the number of people and compare the results. If the results are the same, the answer is yes. In the process of answering the question in this way it is necessary to find an additional bit of information that was not asked for— the number of trees and the number of people.

There is another way of answering the question which does not require that we find this additional bit of information. We could ask that the people walk out into the yard and that each stand by a tree, but stipulate that no two people stand by the same tree. Then if every tree has a person next to it and there are no people or trees left over, we can answer the original question with a yes.

The second procedure tells us that the notion of two collections having *the same number of elements* does not depend upon the notion of the *number of elements* in either collection. This independence is important, since it enables us to ask whether two sets have the same number of elements even when we are not able to answer the question about the number of elements in the sets.

Let us consider a second example. Let Z again be the set of natural numbers and let E be the set of even natural numbers. We can ask if Z and E have the same number of elements. Here only the second of the two methods used above is applicable. This points out the importance of the independence of the notions of *the same number of elements* in two sets and *the number of elements* in a set. There still seems to be a kind of ambiguity, however, when we consider the following two statements with their arguments.

(1) Z has more elements than E, since all elements of E are in Z, but not all elements of Z are in E.

(2) Z and E have the same number of elements, since each element of Z can be placed next to its double in E, and this exactly uses up the elements in both sets.

Which answer is correct? Many hours have been spent in futile arguing over this point. The difficulty is that though the phrase "the same number of elements" has a well accepted (and unambiguous) meaning when applied to "finite" sets, it has not any well accepted (to the layman) meaning when applied to "non-finite" sets. Thus, we must define what is meant when we say two sets have the same number of elements. Only then, in the light of the definition, will we be in a position to answer the question of whether Z and E have the same number of elements. Theoretically, we are free to define this phrase in any way that pleases us. Practically, however, we insist that our definition be such that when it is applied to finite sets it yields the results generally accepted.

We make a preliminary definition which utilizes the notion of a 1 to 1 mapping of a set onto another (see p. 17).

DEFINITION.   *Two sets A and B are equivalent if there exists a 1 to 1 mapping of A onto B. When A and B are equivalent we shall write* $A \sim B$.

(The notion of equivalence used here is the same as that used in Appendix A, but is not the same as any other notion of equivalence used in this text. In particular, it is not the same as that introduced in Chapter III.)

The proof of the next lemma is left as an exercise.

LEMMA.   (i) *For every set A*, $A \sim A$;

(ii) *For any sets A and B*, $A \sim B$ *implies* $B \sim A$;

(iii) *For any sets A, B, and C,*

$$A \sim B, \ B \sim C \ \text{implies} \ A \sim C.$$

We now make the following definition.

DEFINITION.   *Two sets have the same number of elements if and only if they are equivalent.*

We see immediately that the argument in statement (2), p. 56, regarding Z and E is the one we accept. Thus, we say that Z and E do have the same number of elements. The 1 to 1 mapping specified in statement (2) is given by f, where $f(n) = 2n$ for all n in Z.

2. Finite Sets and Finite Cardinal Numbers

We introduce the following auxiliary sets.

$$S_1 = \{1\},$$
$$S_2 = \{1, 2\},$$
$$S_3 = \{1, 2, 3\},$$
$$\vdots$$
$$S_n = \{1, 2, \cdots, n\},$$
$$\vdots$$

Using these sets we make the following definition.

DEFINITION. *A nonempty set is finite if and only if it is equivalent to S_n for some n. The empty set is also finite.*

Thus, for example, the sets A = $\{\Delta, *\}$ and B = $\{5, 6, 7, 8, 9\}$ are finite, since A $\sim S_2$ and B $\sim S_5$.

It is important to know that a set cannot be equivalent to more than one S_n. To prove this we first show that for $n \neq m$ the sets S_n and S_m are not equivalent.

LEMMA. *If $n \neq m$, then S_n and S_m are not equivalent.*

Proof: We assume the lemma to be false and derive a contradiction. Let M be the set of all natural numbers n for which $S_m \sim S_n$ for some $m \neq n$. By our assumption, M is not empty and therefore has a smallest element, say r. Since it is clear that S_1 is not equivalent to S_m for $m \neq 1$ we know that $r > 1$. Let f be a 1 to 1 mapping of S_r onto S_m and define the mapping g from S_{r-1} to S_{m-1} by

$$g(a) = \begin{cases} f(a) \text{ for } f(a) < f(r); \\ f(a) - 1 \text{ for } f(a) > f(r). \end{cases}$$

It can be easily shown (see exercise 2, p. 61) that g is a 1 to 1 mapping of S_{r-1} onto S_{m-1}, so we have $S_{r-1} \sim S_{m-1}$. But $0 < r - 1 < r$, and this contradicts the definition of r. Hence, the assumption that M is not empty is false, and the lemma is proved.

Thus, if A $\sim S_n$ and A $\sim S_m$, we know by properties (ii) and

(iii) of $\sim$ that $S_n \sim S_m$, and therefore by the lemma just proved $n = m$. This argument justifies the uniqueness of the cardinal number of a finite set as given in the next definition.

DEFINITION.   *A set is said to have the (finite) cardinal number n if the set is equivalent to* S_n. *(We also say of such a set that it has cardinality n.) The empty set is said to have cardinality "zero."*

The sets $A = \{\Delta, *\}$ and $B = \{5, 6, 7, 8, 9\}$ have the cardinal numbers 2 and 5, respectively. At the moment we do not know if the set Z has a finite cardinal number. In the next section we shall prove that it does not.

3. Infinite Sets

Before proving that Z is not finite we prove a lemma.

LEMMA.   *Let q be any natural number, and let* Z_q *be the set of all other natural numbers. Then* $Z \sim Z_q$.

Proof: We need only exhibit a 1 to 1 mapping of Z onto Z_q. Such a mapping is f where

$$f(n) = \begin{cases} n \text{ for } n < q; \\ n + 1 \text{ for } n \geq q. \end{cases}$$

We can picture f as follows:

$$Z = \{1, 2, 3, \cdots, q - 1, q, q + 1, q + 2, \cdots\},$$
$$Z_q = \{1, 2, 3, \cdots, q - 1, q + 1, q + 2, q + 3, \cdots\}.$$

Clearly, f is a 1 to 1 mapping of Z onto Z_q, and the lemma is proved.

COROLLARY.   *If* $q_1, \cdots, q_n$ *are distinct natural numbers and* $Z_{q_1, \ldots, q_n}$ *is the set of all other natural numbers, then* $Z \sim Z_{q_1, \ldots, q_n}$.

We now prove that Z is not finite.

THEOREM. Z *is not equivalent to* S_n *for any n.*

Proof: Suppose $Z \sim S_n$ for some n. Then there is a 1 to 1 mapping f of Z onto S_n. For some q in Z we have $f(q) = n$. Define a mapping

g of Z_q to S_{n-1} (it is clear that $n > 1$) by

$$g(a) = f(a) \text{ for } a \text{ in } Z_q.$$

This is obviously a 1 to 1 mapping of Z_q onto S_{n-1}. Hence, $Z_q \sim S_{n-1}$. Since, by the lemma, $Z \sim Z_q$ we conclude from the transitivity of $\sim$ that $Z \sim S_{n-1}$. But then since $Z \sim S_n$ and $Z \sim S_{n-1}$, we must have $n = n - 1$, which is absurd. Therefore, the supposition that $Z \sim S_n$ for some n is false.

This theorem proves that Z is not finite. In accordance with the following definition we have shown that Z is "infinite."

DEFINITION. *A set which is not finite is called infinite.*

We extend the notion of cardinal number to those sets which are equivalent to Z.

DEFINITION. *A set is said to have cardinal number* $\aleph_0$ *(read "aleph nought") if it is equivalent to* Z. (Such sets are also said to have *cardinality* $\aleph_0$. They are also sometimes referred to as "enumerable," "denumerable," or "countable" sets. Since various authors sometimes subsume finite sets under these terms, the reader is cautioned to check each author to establish how the words are used.)

The sets $A = \{2, 4, 6, 8, \cdots\}$ and $B = \{1, 3, 5, 7, \cdots\}$, and Z itself, all have cardinal number $\aleph_0$. It is easy to see that every set with cardinal number $\aleph_0$ is infinite. The converse proposition is false, as will be seen in Appendix A.

We show next that Z and R are equivalent. Arrange the elements of R in a rectangular array as shown on the right. The nth row contains all those elements a/n, where a has no factor greater than 1 in common with n. We now map Z onto R as shown below. The subscript indicates which element of Z maps

1/1	2/1	3/1	4/1	$\cdots$
1/2	3/2	5/2	7/2	$\cdots$
1/3	2/3	4/3	5/3	$\cdots$
1/4	3/4	5/4	7/4	$\cdots$
		$\cdots$		

onto the given element of R. Thus, $(a/b)_k$ means k maps onto a/b.

$(1/1)_1 \rightarrow (2/1)_2 \quad (3/1)_6 \rightarrow (4/1)_7 \quad (5/1)_{15} \rightarrow (6/1)_{16}$

$(1/2)_3 \quad (3/2)_5 \quad (5/2)_8 \quad (7/2)_{14} \quad (9/2)_{17}$

$(1/3)_4 \quad (2/3)_9 \quad (4/3)_{13} \quad (5/3)_{18}$

$(1/4)_{10} \quad (3/4)_{12}$

$(1/5)_{11}$

$\ldots$

It is quite clear that the mapping described is a 1 to 1 mapping of Z onto R. There is no nice way of describing this mapping by means of a formula.

The set of all "points in the plane" which are at the same time above the x-axis by an integral distance and to the right of the y-axis by an integral distance also has cardinal number $\aleph_0$. This set of points and the mapping of the set onto Z is indicated in the following diagram, in which the dots are the points of the set, and the numbers attached to the dots are the elements of Z associated with them under the 1 to 1 mapping.

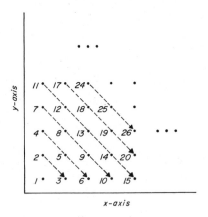

Since the set $Z \times Z$ is in obvious 1 to 1 correspondence with the points of the plane described above, we may conclude that $Z \times Z \sim Z$. That is, the cardinality of $Z \times Z$ is $\aleph_0$.

● EXERCISES

1. Prove the lemma in Section 1.

2. Explain by means of diagrams the mapping g introduced in the proof of the lemma in Section 2.

3. Prove the corollary to the lemma in Section 3.

4. Why is it "clear" that $n > 1$ in the proof of the theorem in Section 3?

5. Prove that the set $\{1, 3, 5, 7, \cdots\}$ has cardinal number $\aleph_0$.

6. (a) Prove that every subset of a finite set is finite.
(b) Prove that if a set has an infinite subset then the set is infinite. [*Hint:* For part (a) let A be a nonempty finite set, $A \sim S_k$. If $k = 1$, the proposition is true. Suppose the proposition is true for $k \leq n$. Consider $A \sim S_{n+1}$. Prove that each nonempty subset of A other than A itself is equivalent to a subset of S_n.]

7. Prove that the number of prime numbers is infinite.
[*Hint:* Assume there are only finitely many primes, say $p_1, \cdots, p_n$. By exercise 7(a), p. 37, the number $q = p_1 \cdots p_n + 1$ contains a prime factor p. Since $p_1, \cdots, p_n$ are all the primes, we must have p a factor of $p_1 \cdots p_n$. Hence, by Lemma 2, p. 35, p must divide 1. This is not possible, so the assumption is false. This proof was given by Euclid in his *Elements*.]

8. Prove that the set $(Z \times Z) \times Z$ has cardinality $\aleph_0$.

9. Prove that if A and B are finite sets, then $A \times B$ is a finite set.

10. Prove that if A is a set of cardinality $\aleph_0$, then $A \times A$ has cardinality $\aleph_0$.

11. Prove that if A is infinite, then the set of all mappings of A into A is infinite. [*Hint:* Consider the subset of "constant" mappings and use exercise 6(b) above.]

12. (a) Prove that a finite set is not equivalent to a proper subset of itself.
(b) Use part (a) to prove that Z is not finite.

IV Interlude, In Which the Way is Prepared

At the start of Chapter III we expressed some dissatisfaction with the system $(Z; +, \cdot ; <)$ on the grounds that not all equations of the form $ax = b$, for a and b in Z, were solvable in Z. Hence, we proceeded to extend this system to a system in which all such equations were solvable. There are various reasons of a similar nature which make us dissatisfied with the system $(R; +, \cdot ; <)$ constructed in the last chapter. For instance, not all equations of the form $a + x = b$ are solvable in $(R; +, \cdot ; <)$, when a, b are in R. Also, not all equations of the form $x^2 = a$, for a in R, are solvable in R. Ultimately we wish to find a system in which both kinds of equations are always solvable. It is a matter of choice whether we make the system $(R; +, \cdot ; <)$ grow into a larger one in which equations such as $a + x = b$ are always solvable and then make the new system grow so that equations such as $x^2 = a$ (a in R) are always solvable, or whether we reverse the order. In the one case we construct from the positive rational numbers the set of all rational numbers and then proceed to the set of all real numbers. In the other case we proceed from the positive rational numbers to all nonnegative real numbers and then to *all* real numbers. In this text we follow the latter order.

In this chapter we attempt to give some motivation for the methods to be used in the next chapter. Also, we give preliminary discussions of some technical matters which will be needed.

IV.1. Square Roots in R

The number r in R has a *square root* in R if the equation $x^2 = r$ has a solution in R. Any solution of this equation is called a *square root of r*.

THEOREM. *If a positive integer is not the square of a positive integer it is not the square of a rational number.*

Proof (Due to Richard Dedekind.) Let d be an integer, and suppose $x^2 = d$ is solvable in R but not in Z. Then there are integers r', s' ($s' \neq 1$) such that $(r'/s')^2 = d$. Let r, s be such a pair, s being as small as possible. Then

$$d = r^2/s^2. \tag{1}$$

Also there exists a positive integer λ such that

$$\lambda^2 < d < (\lambda + 1)^2. \tag{2}$$

From (1) and (2) we see that $ds - \lambda r$ and $r - \lambda s$ are defined and that

$$r - \lambda s < s.$$

Further,

$$(ds - \lambda r)^2/(r - \lambda s)^2 = d.$$

But this contradicts the definition of s as being the smallest s' such that $(r'/s')^2 = d$. Hence, if $x^2 = d$ is not solvable in Z, it cannot be solved in R either.

● EXERCISES

1. In the proof of the above theorem carry out the details showing that:
   (a) there exists a positive integer λ such that (2) holds;
   (b) $ds - \lambda r$ and $r - \lambda s$ are defined;
   (c) $r - \lambda s < s$;
   (d) $(ds - \lambda r)^2/(r - \lambda s)^2 = d$.

2.* Using the above theorem show that $x^2 = 2$ is not solvable in R.

3. Exercise 2 shows that $x^2 = r$ for r in R does not necessarily have a solution in R. Prove that when this equation is solvable the solution is unique.

4. Deduce the above theorem from the theorem on p. 35. [*Hint:* If $(r/s)^2 = d$, where r and s have no common factor greater than 1, then $r^2 = ds^2$ and, when d is a nonsquare, deduce that r and s do have a common factor greater than 1.]

IV.2. Denseness

Let L be a linear order relation in a set S. If s, s', s'' are three elements of S such that

$$sLs'' \text{ and } s''Ls',$$

then we say that s'' is *between s and s'* (with respect to L). If between any two elements of S there is a third element of S, we say that S is *dense with respect to* L. A subset S' of S is said to be *dense in* S if between any two elements of S there is an element of S'.

LEMMA 1. R *is dense with respect to* $<$.

Proof: See exercise 2, p. 65.

Not only is R dense, but the following lemma is true.

LEMMA 2. *If m is in Z and r, r' are in R, r $<$ r', there exists a "finite chain" of elements of R, say $r_1, \cdots, r_n$, such that:*
  (i) $r = r_1 < r_2 < \cdots < r_{n-1} < r_n = r'$;
  (ii) $r_2 - r_1 < 1/m, r_3 - r_2 < 1/m, \cdots, r_n - r_{n-1} < 1/m$.

Proof: See exercise 3, p. 65.

LEMMA 3. *Let r be in R and m be in Z. Then there is an s in R whose square lies between r and r + 1/m; that is, $r < s^2 < r + 1/m$.*

Proof: Let A be the set of all rational numbers whose squares are less than r, and let B be the set of all rational numbers whose squares are greater than or equal to r. (Imagining the rational numbers strung out according to $<$, the accompanying pictures might prove helpful.)

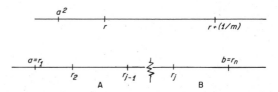

Let a, b be in A, B, respectively, with $b^2 > r$. Then $a^2 < r < b^2$. Let m' be in Z, and let $r_1, r_2, \cdots, r_n$ be a finite chain from a to b such that

$$a = r_1 < r_2 < \cdots < r_n = b,$$
$$r_2 - r_1 < 1/m', \cdots, r_n - r_{n-1} < 1/m'.$$

(Note that n depends upon m'.) Now there is a smallest i for which $r_i^2 > r$. Let j be this smallest i. Then

$$r_{j-1}^2 \leq r,$$
$$r_j^2 > r.$$

Now since $r_j - r_{j-1} < 1/m'$, we have

$$r_j < r_{j-1} + 1/m',$$

and therefore

$$r_j^2 < r_{j-1}^2 + 2r_{j-1}/m' + 1/m'^2 \leq r + (2bm' + 1)/m'^2.$$

By exercise 10, p. 53, if we choose m' sufficiently large, then $r_j^2 < r + 1/m$. Since $r_j^2 > r$, this completes the proof.

COROLLARY 1. *Between any two numbers in* R *there is a square of a number in* R. *That is, the set of squares of elements of* R *is dense in* R *with respect to* $<$.

COROLLARY 2. *If* r *has no square root in* R, *then the class* A *as defined in the proof of the lemma has no greatest number, and the class* B *has no least number.*

These corollaries are to be proved in exercises 5 and 6, below.

● EXERCISES

1. Is the system $(\mathbf{Z}; <)$ dense with respect to $<$?

2. Prove Lemma 1.

3. Prove Lemma 2.

4. Prove that $(a + c)/(b + d)$ is between a/b and c/d when $a/b \neq c/d$ (a, b, c, d are in Z).

5. Prove Corollary 1 to Lemma 3.

6. Prove Corollary 2 to Lemma 3.

7.* (a) Justify the steps in the following proof that there is no largest rational number whose square is less than r. Given x in R, $x^2 < r$ and $y = x(x^2 + 3r)/(3x^2 + r)$.

   (i) The numbers $y, r - x^2, 2x(r - x^2)/(3x^2 + r), (r - x^2)^3/(3x^2 + r)^2$ are defined in R;

(ii) The equation $y = z + x$ is solvable for z in R; in fact, $z = 2x(r - x^2)/(3x^2 + r)$ is the solution;

(iii) The equation $r = y^2 + z$ is solvable for z in R; in fact, $z = (r - x^2)^3/(3x^2 + r)^2$ is the solution;

(iv) $x < y$ and $y^2 < r$;

(v) Conclusion follows.

(b) Do the same to show that there is no smallest rational whose square is greater than r. Given x in R, $r < x^2$ and $y = x(x^2 + 3r)/(3x^2 + r)$.

(i) The numbers y, $x^2 - r$, $2x(x^2 - r)/(3x^2 + r)$, $(x^2 - r)^3/(3x^2 + r)^2$ are defined in R;

(ii) The equation $y + z = x$ is solvable for z in R; in fact, $z = 2x(x^2 - r)/(3x^2 + r)$ is the solution;

(iii) The equation $r + z = y^2$ is solvable for z in R; in fact, $z = (x^2 - r)^3/(3x^2 + r)^2$ is the solution.

(iv) $y < x$ and $y^2 > r$;

(v) Conclusion follows.

This exercise includes a second proof of Corollary 2 above. Note that by means of the formulas given in this exercise we can readily compute a rational square closer to r than a given rational square (providing the given one is not equal to r).

IV.3. Sequences

In our preceding work we have met strings of numbers such as

$$1, 2, 3, 4, 5, 6, \cdots ;$$
$$2, 4, 6, 8, 10, 12, \cdots ;$$
$$2, 3, 5, 7, 11, 13, \cdots .$$

Such strings are called *sequences*. In general, if S is a set, a string of elements of the set

$$s_1, s_2, s_3, \cdots$$

is called a *sequence in* S. The individual s_i are called the *terms* of the sequence.

We do not insist that all the terms of a sequence be distinct.

For example,

$$2, 1, 2, 1, 2, 1, \cdots ;$$
$$1, 1, 1, 1, 1, 1, \cdots ;$$
$$1, 2, 2, 3, 3, 3, \cdots ;$$

are sequences in Z.

A sequence in S may be thought of as a listing of (not necessarily distinct) elements of S in such a way that:

(i) there is a first element;

(ii) given any element in the listing there is a next following element in the listing;

(iii) given any element in the listing other than the first there is a next preceding element in the listing.

The following listings of elements in Z are *not* sequences, because in each instance at least one of the properties mentioned for a sequence is violated.

(a) $1, 5, 4, 10, 9, 15, 14, 20$; *because it's finite violates ii*

(b) $2, 4, 6, 8, \cdots, 1, 3, 5, 7, \cdots$; *violates 3*

(c) $\cdots, 7, 6, 5, 4, 3, 2, 1, 2, 3, 4, 5, \cdots$. *violates 1*

The listing in (a) satisfies properties (i) and (iii), but fails to satisfy property (ii). The listing in (b) satisfies properties (i) and (ii) but fails to satisfy property (iii). The listing in (c) satisfies properties (ii) and (iii) but fails to satisfy property (i).

Let $S = \{\alpha, \beta, \gamma, \delta\}$. Then the following listings of elements of S are sequences in S.

(1) $\alpha, \beta, \gamma, \delta, \beta, \gamma, \delta, \beta, \gamma, \delta, \cdots$;

(2) $\beta, \gamma, \delta, \beta, \gamma, \delta, \beta, \gamma, \delta, \cdots$;

(3) $\beta, \delta, \gamma, \beta, \delta, \gamma, \beta, \delta, \cdots$;

(4) $\beta, \delta, \beta, \gamma, \delta, \gamma, \delta, \gamma, \delta \cdots$;

(5) $\gamma, \beta, \delta, \delta, \delta, \delta, \cdots$.

With the exception of (1) and (5) we may obtain each of these sequences by deleting terms of the sequence immediately above it. Thus, we can get (2) from (1) by deleting the first term; (3) from (2) by deleting the second, fourth, sixth, eighth, $\cdots$ terms; (4) from (3) by deleting the third, fifth, seventh, tenth,$\cdots$ terms. However, we cannot obtain (5) from (4) by deleting terms, since in (4) we do not have a β following any γ. We say that (2) is a subsequence of (1), (3) is a subsequence of (2), (4) is a subsequence of (3), but (5) is not a subsequence of (4).

In general, any sequence obtained from a sequence by deleting terms of the sequence is called a subsequence of the sequence. Also each sequence is a subsequence of itself (deleting no terms).

● EXERCISES

1. Let $S = \{\delta, \Delta, \lambda, *\}$. Find four sequences in S.

2. Find a subsequence of each of the sequences found in number 1.

3. Suppose $a_1, a_2, a_3, \cdots$ is a subsequence of $b_1, b_2, b_3, \cdots$, which in turn is a subsequence of $c_1, c_2, c_3, \cdots$. Is $a_1, a_2, a_3, \cdots$ a subsequence of $c_1, c_2, c_3, \cdots$? Explain.

4. Find ten distinct subsequences of the sequence $1,2,1,2,1,2,\cdots$.

5. Give three examples of sequences which have the sequence $\{n/(n+1)\}$ as a subsequence.

6. Show that every sequence in $\{\alpha, \beta, \gamma, \delta\}$, no term of which is α, is a subsequence of (1), p. 67.

IV.4. Inequality Notation

In the sequel we shall often be concerned with the closeness of pairs of numbers. To work with this notion conveniently it behooves us to introduce a workable notation for the situation described by the phrase: "The numbers a and b are within c of each other." As a first approximation we translate the phrase to obtain:

$$a = b, \text{ or}$$
$$a < b \text{ and } b - a < c, \text{ or} \qquad \text{(I)}$$
$$b < a \text{ and } a - b < c.$$

However, it is not convenient to write these three lines each time they are appropriate. We shorten them to the assertion:

$$a < b + c \text{ and } b < a + c. \qquad \text{(II)}$$

It is left to the reader to prove the equivalence of formulations (I) and (II). We make one final modification and write the following definition.

DEFINITION. $|a, b| < c$ *if and only if* (II).

Note that $|a, b| < c$ is a single phrase and that we have *not* defined the expression to the left of the inequality sign independently. We shall read $|a, b| < c$ as "a is within c of b" or as "a and b are within c of each other."

We now state and prove two lemmas.

LEMMA 1. (The triangle inequality.) *If* $|r, r'| < d$ *and* $|r', r''| < e$, *then* $|r, r''| < d + e$.

Proof: Because $|r, r'| < d$ and $|r', r''| < e$ we have

$$r < r' + d,$$
$$r' < r + d,$$
$$r' < r'' + e,$$
$$r'' < r' + e.$$

Hence,

$$r < r' + d < (r'' + e) + d = r'' + (d + e)$$

and

$$r'' < r' + e < (r + d) + e = r + (d + e).$$

But $r < r'' + (d + e)$ and $r'' < r + (d + e)$ yield $|r, r''| < d + e$, and the lemma is proved.

LEMMA 2. *If* $|a, b| < 1/m$, *for all* m, *then* $a = b$.

Proof: From $|a, b| < 1/m$ we have

$$a < b + 1/m \text{ and } b < a + 1/m.$$

We shall show that $a < b$ and $b < a$ both lead to a contradiction. Suppose $a < b$. Then $a + c = b$ for some c. Hence, $b = a + c < a + 1/m$. This implies $c < 1/m$ or $mc < 1$. This must hold for all m. But this contradicts the Archimedean property. Hence, $a < b$ is false. Similarly, $b < a$ is false, and the lemma is proved.

● EXERCISES

1. Prove the equivalence of (I) and (II), p. 68.

2. In the proof of Lemma 2 carry out the details showing that b cannot be less than a.

3.* Prove $|a, b| < c$ if and only if $|b, a| < c$.

4.* Prove, when $|a, b| < c$:

(i) $|a + d, b + d| < c$;

(ii) $|ad, bd| < cd$;

(iii) $|a - d, b - d| < c$ when $d < \min \{a, b\}$.

5.* Define $|a, b| > c$ to mean $\max \{a, b\} > c + \min \{a, b\}$. Show:

(i) $|a, b| > c$ if and only if $|b, a| > c$.

(ii) If $|a, b| > c$, then $|a + d, b + d| > c$.

(iii) If $|a, b| > c$, then $|ad, bd| > cd$.

(iv) If $|a, b| > c$, then $|a, b| < c$ is false.

IV.5. Limits of Sequences

The sequence r_1, r_2, r_3, $\cdots$ in R is designated by $\{r_n\}$. As we have observed, it is not necessary that the terms of the sequence be all distinct. In fact, they may be all equal. But this also is not necessary. In this section we shall systematically use r, $\bar{r}$, r_j, and so on for elements of R, and we shall use m, m_o, N, n, and so on for elements of Z (that is, Z_R)

DEFINITION. (a) *The sequence $\{r_n\}$ converges to r, symbolized* $r_n \to r$, *if for each m in Z there is an N such that when $n >$ N then* $|r, r_n| < 1/m$.

(b) *If $\{r_n\}$ converges to r, we call r a limit of the sequence.*

Note that the value of N depends upon that of m. Generally, the larger m is the larger N must be.

Before giving some examples we prove a lemma which guarantees that a sequence can converge to only one limit.

LEMMA. *If $r_n \to r$ and $r_n \to r'$, then $r = r'$.*

Proof: Since $r_n \to r$: given $2m$ there is an N such that for $n >$ N we have $|r, r_n| < 1/(2m)$. Since $r_n \to r'$: given $2m$ there is an N' such that for $n >$ N' we have $|r', r_n| < 1/(2m)$. Thus, for $n > \max(N, N')$ we have

$$|r, r_n| < 1/(2m) \text{ and } |r', r_n| < 1/(2m).$$

Hence, by Lemma 1, Section IV.4, and exercise 3, p. 70, we must have $|r, r'| < 1/m$. But this is true for all m, and therefore by Lemma 2, Section IV.4, $r = r'$.

● EXAMPLES

   (a) If $r_n = 1$ for all n, then $r_n \to 1$.
   (b) If $r_{2n} = 1$, $r_{2n-1} = n/(n+1)$, then $r_n \to 1$.
This sequence begins $1/2$, 1, $2/3$, 1, $3/4$, 1, $4/5$, 1, $5/6$, $1, \cdots$. In order to show $r_n \to 1$ we must show that for a given m there is an N such that when $n > N$ then the two inequalities $r_n < r + 1/m$, $r < r_n + 1/m$ hold. For each m choose $N = 2m$. Then if $n > N$, either $n = 2k$ or $n = 2k - 1$, where $k > m$. When $n = 2k$ we have $r_n = 1$, so $r_n = 1 < 1 + 1/m = r + 1/m$ and $r = 1 < 1 + 1/m = r_n + 1/m$. When $n = 2k - 1$ we have $r_n = k/(k+1)$, so $r = 1 = k/(k+1) + 1/(k+1) < r_n + 1/m$ and $r_n = k/(k+1) < 1 = r < r + 1/m$.
   (c) Making use of exercise 14(b), p. 54, we find the sequence

$$r + b/a, r + b/a^2, r + b/a^3, \cdots$$

converges to r when $a > 1$.
   (d) Let $Q_n = (1 - q^{n+1})/(1 - q)$, where $q < 1$. Then $Q_n \to 1/(1-q)$. [Noting that $Q_n = 1 + q + \cdots + q^n$ (see exercise 16, p. 54) we can write $1 + q + \cdots + q^n = 1/(1-q) - q^{n+1}/(1-q) \to 1/(1-q)$ when $q < 1$.]
   (e) If $r_n = 1/n$, then $\{r_n\}$ does not converge to any element of R. Suppose $r_n \to r$. Choose m such that $1/m < r/2$. Then there is an N for which $n > N$ implies $1/n < r + 1/m$ and $r < 1/n + 1/m$. But for $n > 2/r$ we have $r = r/2 + r/2 > 1/n + 1/m$, and the second inequality is violated. Hence, no such r exists.

● EXERCISES

   1. Prove $r_n \to 1$ in example (a) above.

   2. Prove the assertions made in example (c) above.

   3. Prove the assertions made in example (d) above.

4. Let $r_1 = 1$ and $r_{n+1} = 1 + 1/2 + \cdots + (1/2)^n$ for $n \geq 1$. Does $\{r_n\}$ converge?

5. Let $r_1 = 1/2$, $r_2 = 1$, $r_{3n} = 1$, $r_{3n+1} = n/(n + 1)$, $r_{3n+2} = (n+1)/n$ for $n \geq 1$. Does $\{r_n\}$ converge, and if so, what is its limit?

6. Suppose $r_n \to r$ and $r'_n \to r$. Show that the sequence $r_1, r'_1, r_2, r'_2, r_3, r'_3, \cdots$ converges to r.

7. Prove that the sequence $1, (1/2)^2, (1/3)^2, (1/4)^2, \cdots$ does not converge to any element of R. *It converges to 0.*

8. Prove that the sequence $1 + 1$, $1 + (1/2)^2$, $1 + (1/3)^2$, $1 + (1/4)^2, \cdots$ converges to 1.

9.* Prove that there exists a sequence $\{r_n\}$ such that $r_n^2 \to 2$.

IV.6. Bounds and Cauchy Sequences

DEFINITION. (a) *The sequence* $\{r_n\}$ *is said to be bounded above if there is a number* M (*not necessarily in* Z) *such that* $r_n \leq$ M *for all* n. *Such an* M *is called an upper bound of the sequence.*

(b) *The sequence* $\{r_n\}$ *is said to be bounded below if there is a number* M (*not necessarily in* Z) *such that* M $\leq r_n$ *for all* n. *Such an* M *is called a lower bound of the sequence.*

(c) *The sequence* $\{r_n\}$ *is said to be bounded if it has an upper and a lower bound.*

LEMMA 1. *Every convergent sequence is bounded.*

Proof: Let $\{r_n\}$ be a convergent sequence with limit r.

(a) Since $r_n \to r$: given $m = 1$ there is an N such that if $n > $ N, then $|r, r_n| < 1$. Define M by

$$M = \max(r + 1, r_1, r_2, \cdots, r_N).$$

Then certainly for $1 \leq i \leq $ N we have $r_i \leq$ M. For $i > $ N we have $|r, r_i| < 1$, and therefore

$$r_i < r + 1 \leq M.$$

This proves M is an upper bound of $\{r_n\}$.

(b) Since $r_n \to r$: given $m > 2/r$ there is an N such that if $n > $ N, then $|r, r_n| < r/2$. Define M' by

$$M' = \min(r/2, r_1, \cdots, r_N).$$

Then certainly for $1 \leq i \leq N$ we have $M' \leq r_i$. For $i > N$ we have $|r, r_i| < r/2$, and therefore

$$r < r_i + r/2.$$

But this means $M' \leq r/2 < r_i$. This proves M' is a lower bound of $\{r_n\}$.

We now define a class of sequences which will play an important role in the sequel.

DEFINITION. *The sequence $\{r_n\}$ is said to be a Cauchy sequence if: given m there exists an N such that when n and n' are both greater than N, then*

$$|r_n, r_{n'}| < 1/m.$$

We shall call a sequence *Cauchy* if it is a Cauchy sequence.

LEMMA 2. *Every convergent sequence is Cauchy.*

Proof: Let $\{r_n\}$ be a convergent sequence with limit r. Then given $2m$ there is an N such that when $n > N$ then $|r, r_n| < 1/(2m)$. Suppose $n' > N$ also. Then $|r, r_{n'}| < 1/(2m)$. Hence, by Lemma 1, Section IV.4 and exercise 3, p. 70, $|r_n, r_{n'}| < 1/m$. This completes the proof.

LEMMA 3. *Every Cauchy sequence is bounded above.*

Proof: Let $\{r_n\}$ be a Cauchy sequence. Then for $m = 1$ there is an N such that when $n > N$, $n' > N$ then $|r_n, r_{n'}| < 1$. Define M by

$$M = \max\{r_{N+1} + 1, r_1, \cdots, r_N\}.$$

Then certainly for $1 \leq i \leq N$, $r_i \leq M$. For $i > N$, $|r_{N+1}, r_i| < 1$, and therefore $r_i < r_{N+1} + 1 \leq M$. This completes the proof.

One might feel that "bounded above" in this lemma could be replaced by "bounded." This cannot be done, as we can see by considering the sequence

$$1, 1/2, 1/3, 1/4, 1/5, \cdots .$$

This sequence is Cauchy, but has no lower bound. (No lower bound in R that is. If we had 0 or negative numbers the situation would be different.)

We have seen that all convergent sequences are Cauchy. The converse is false, since there are Cauchy sequences which do not converge. For example, the sequence $1, 1/2, 1/3, 1/4, \cdots$ does not converge. (If it did, by Lemma 1, it would have a lower bound, which it doesn't.) We shall give a less trivial example following the next lemma.

LEMMA 4. *If $r_n \to r$, then $r_n^2 \to r^2$.*

Proof: We need to show that for given m there is an N such that $n > N$ implies $\left| r_n^2, r^2 \right| < 1/m$. Thus, fix m. Then, since $r_n \to r$, for each A there is an N' such that $n > N'$ implies $\left| r, r_n \right| < 1/(Am)$. By exercise 4, p. 70, this yields

$$\begin{aligned} \left| r^2, rr_n \right| &< r/(Am), \\ \left| rr_n, r_n^2 \right| &< r_n/(Am). \end{aligned}$$

Now Lemma 1, Section IV.4 gives

$$\left| r^2, r_n^2 \right| < (r + r_n)/(Am).$$

We need only choose $A > r + r_n$ to make the right side less than $1/m$. Lemma 1 of this section guarantees that we can do this. Now take N to be the N' corresponding to such an A, and the proof is complete.

You might wonder, in connection with Lemma 4, whether we can deduce the convergence of $\{r_n\}$ from the knowledge that $r_n^2 \to r$. The answer is no. This is seen as follows. Choose a sequence $\{r_n^2\}$ such that $r_n^2 \to 2$ (see exercise 9, p. 72). If $r_n \to r$ for some r, then, by Lemma 4, $r_n^2 \to r^2$. But by the uniqueness of limits, proved in Section IV.5, we would then have $r^2 = 2$. This contradicts exercise 2, p. 63.

The above shows us that when $r_n^2 \to 2$ the sequence $\{r_n\}$ does not converge. However, since when $r_n^2 \to 2$ the sequence $\{r_n^2\}$ is Cauchy, the following lemma shows us that the sequence $\{r_n\}$ is also Cauchy.

LEMMA 5. $\{r_n^2\}$ *Cauchy implies* $\{r_n\}$ *Cauchy.*

Proof: Let m be given. Choose m' such that $1/m' < 1/m^2$. Since $\{r_n^2\}$ is Cauchy, we may choose N such that $n > N$ and $q > N$ imply

$$\left| r_n^2, r_q^2 \right| < 1/m'.$$

Then

$$r_n^2 < r_q^2 + 1/m' < r_q^2 + 2r_q/m + 1/m^2 = (r_q + 1/m)^2,$$

and

$$r_q^2 < r_n^2 + 1/m' < r_n^2 + 2r_n/m + 1/m^2 = (r_n + 1/m)^2.$$

Hence

$$r_n < r_q + 1/m$$

and

$$r_q < r_n + 1/m,$$

and therefore

$$|r_n, r_q| < 1/m,$$

and the lemma is proved.

● EXERCISES

1. Prove that the sequence $1, 1/2, 1/3, 1/4, \cdots$ is:
(a) Cauchy;
(b) without lower bound;
(c) not convergent.

2. Exhibit a sequence with no lower *and* no upper bound.

3. Sketch a diagram indicating the implications between the following:
(a) $\{r_n\}$ is bounded;
(b) $\{r_n\}$ is Cauchy;
(c) $\{r_n\}$ is convergent;
(d) $\{r_n^2\}$ is convergent;
(e) $\{r_n^2\}$ is Cauchy;
(f) $\{r_n^2\}$ is bounded.

4.* (a) Let $\{r_n\}$, $\{r_n'\}$ be Cauchy sequences. Show that for each m there is an N such that for $n > N$, $n' > N$ we have both $|r_n, r_{n'}| < 1/m$ and $|r_n', r_{n'}'| < 1/m$.
(b) Extend (a) to any finite collection of Cauchy sequences.

5.* (a) Let $\{r_n\}$, $\{r_n'\}$ be Cauchy sequences. Show that there is a constant M such that $r_n < M$ and $r_n' < M$ for all n.
(b) Extend (a) to any finite collection of Cauchy sequences.

6. In the proof of Lemma 1, p. 72, replace part (a) by a proof constructed along the lines of part (b).

7. Let $r_n \to r$ and $r'_n \to r'$. Show that:

(i) the sequence $r_1 + r'_1, r_2 + r'_2, r_3 + r'_3, r_4 + r'_4, \cdots$ converges to $r + r'$;

(ii) the sequence $r_1 r'_1, r_2 r'_2, r_3 r'_3, r_4 r'_4, \cdots$ converges to rr'.

[*Hint:* For part (ii) follow an argument similar to that used in the proof of Lemma 4, p. 74.]

8. Exhibit a sequence of squares which converges to 2. [This problem is considerably harder than it looks and requires considerable ingenuity. It is easy to prove the existence of such a sequence (see exercise 9, p. 72), but difficult to exhibit one. See, however, Appendix D.]

IV.7. Equivalence of Cauchy Sequences

We shall call the Cauchy sequences $\{r_n\}$ and $\{r'_n\}$ *equivalent*, and we shall write $\{r_n\} \sim \{r'_n\}$, when for each m there is an N such that when $n > N$ then $\left| r_n, r'_n \right| < 1/m$.

Remarks. (a) This notion of equivalence and use of the symbol $\sim$ has no connection with the equivalence of ordered pairs as defined in Section III.1. Since we shall not need the earlier notion of equivalence (having already established the positive rational numbers as we have always known them), no ambiguity should arise.

(b) If one or both of the sequences $\{r_n\}$, $\{r'_n\}$ is not a Cauchy sequence, we shall neither say they are equivalent nor say that they are not equivalent. The term equivalent as used here is strictly a relation between Cauchy sequences. Hence, when we write $\{r_n\} \sim \{r'_n\}$ if will be understood, whether explicitly stated or not, that $\{r_n\}$ and $\{r'_n\}$ are *Cauchy* sequences.

In this section we shall discuss Cauchy sequences and the relation of equivalence between Cauchy sequences.

LEMMA 1.   (i) $\{r_n\} \sim \{r_n\}$;

(ii) *If* $\{r_n\} \sim \{r'_n\}$, *then* $\{r'_n\} \sim \{r_n\}$;

(iii) *If* $\{r_n\} \sim \{r'_n\}$ *and* $\{r'_n\} \sim \{r''_n\}$, *then* $\{r_n\} \sim \{r''_n\}$.

Proof: (i) This is immediate, since $\left|r_n, r_n\right| < 1/m$ for all n, m;
        (ii) This is immediate from exercise 3, p. 70.

(iii) Since $\{r_n\} \sim \{r'_n\}$ and $\{r'_n\} \sim \{r''_n\}$, there is an N (see exercise 1, p. 79) such that both $\left|r_n, r'_n\right| < 1/(2m)$ and $\left|r'_n, r''_n\right| < 1/(2m)$ for $n > $ N. Hence, $\left|r_n, r''_n\right| < 1/m$ for $n > $ N. This completes the proof.

COROLLARY. *If* $\{r_n\} \sim \{r''_n\}$ *and* $\{r'_n\} \sim \{r''_n\}$, *then* $\{r_n\} \sim \{r'_n\}$.

LEMMA 2. *If* $\{r_n\}$, $\{r'_n\}$ *are Cauchy sequences, so are* $\{r_n + r'_n\}$, $\{r_n r'_n\}$.

Proof: Let m be an integer.

(a) There is an N such that when $n_1 > $ N, $n_2 > $ N, then $\left|r_{n_1}, r_{n_2}\right| < 1/(2m)$ and $\left|r'_{n_1}, r'_{n_2}\right| < 1/(2m)$. (See exercise 4, p. 75.) Now, by exercise 4(i), p. 70,

$$\left|r_{n_1} + r'_{n_1}, r_{n_2} + r'_{n_1}\right| < 1/(2m)$$

and

$$\left|r_{n_2} + r'_{n_1}, r_{n_2} + r'_{n_2}\right| < 1/(2m),$$

and therefore

$$\left|r_{n_1} + r'_{n_1}, r_{n_2} + r'_{n_2}\right| < 1/m,$$

and we have shown that $\{r_n + r'_n\}$ is a Cauchy sequence.

(b) By exercise 5, p. 75, there is a constant M such that $r_n < $ M, $r'_n < $ M for all n. Also, by exercise 4, p. 75, there is an N such that when $n_1 > $ N, $n_2 > $ N, then

$$\left|r_{n_1}, r_{n_2}\right| < 1/(2m\text{M})$$

and

$$\left|r'_{n_1}, r'_{n_2}\right| < 1/(2m\text{M}).$$

By exercise 4 (ii), p. 70, these yield

$$\left|r_{n_1}r'_{n_1}, r'_{n_1}r_{n_2}\right| < r'_{n_1}/(2m\text{M}) < 1/(2m)$$

and

$$\left|r'_{n_1}r_{n_2}, r_{n_2}r'_{n_2}\right| < r_{n_2}/(2m\text{M}) < 1/(2m).$$

Hence, $\left|r_{n_1}r'_{n_1}, r_{n_2}r'_{n_2}\right| < 1/m$, and $\{r_n r'_n\}$ is a Cauchy sequence.

LEMMA 3. *If* $\{r_n\} \sim \{\bar{r}_n\}$ *and* $\{r'_n\} \sim \{\bar{r}'_n\}$, *then* $\{r_n + r'_n\} \sim \{\bar{r}_n + \bar{r}'_n\}$ *and* $\{r_n r'_n\} \sim \{\bar{r}_n \bar{r}'_n\}$.

Proof: By Lemma 2 all sequences on the right side of the implication are Cauchy, so we need only prove the equivalences. Let m be given.

(a) By exercise 4, p. 75, there is an N such that for $n > N$,

$$\left| r_n, \bar{r}_n \right| < 1/(2m)$$

and

$$\left| r_n', \bar{r}_n' \right| < 1/(2m).$$

Hence

$$\left| r_n + r_n', r_n' + \bar{r}_n \right| < 1/(2m)$$

and

$$\left| \bar{r}_n + r_n', \bar{r}_n + \bar{r}_n' \right| < 1/(2m),$$

and therefore $\left| r_n + r_n', \bar{r}_n + \bar{r}_n' \right| < 1/m$. This proves

$$\{r_n + r_n'\} \sim \{\bar{r}_n + \bar{r}_n'\}.$$

(b) By exercise 5, p. 75, there is an M such that $r_n' < M$, $\bar{r}_n > M$, for all n. By exercise 1, p. 79, there is an N such that, when $n > N$,

$$\left| r_n, \bar{r}_n \right| < 1/(2mM)$$

and

$$\left| r_n', \bar{r}_n' \right| < 1/(2mM).$$

Hence

$$\left| r_n r_n', r_n' \bar{r}_n \right| < r_n'/(2mM) < 1/(2m)$$

and

$$\left| r_n' \bar{r}_n, \bar{r}_n \bar{r}_n' \right| < \bar{r}_n/(2mM) < 1/(2m).$$

Therefore, $\left| r_n r_n', \bar{r}_n \bar{r}_n' \right| < 1/m$ for $n > N$. This proves $\{r_n r_n'\} \sim \{\bar{r}_n \bar{r}_n'\}$ and the lemma.

The sequence $\{r_n\}$, where $r_n = r$ for each n, will be written as $\{r\}$. Such a sequence is called a *constant* sequence. We have the following lemma.

LEMMA 4. $r_n \to r$ *if and only if* $\{r_n\} \sim \{r\}$.

Proof: $r_n \to r$ means that given m there is an N such that $\left| r_n, r \right| < 1/m$ for $n > N$. But this is the definition of $\{r_n\} \sim \{r\}$.

LEMMA 5. *If* $\{r_n\} \sim \{r_n'\}$ *and* $r_n' \to r$, *then* $r_n \to r$.

Proof: Exercise 2, p. 79.

LEMMA 6. *If* $r_n \to r$, $r_n' \to r'$, *then* $r_n + r_n' \to r + r'$ *and* $r_n r_n' \to rr'$.

Proof: By Lemma 4, $\{r_n\} \sim \{r\}$, $\{r'_n\} \sim \{r'\}$. By Lemma 3, $\{r_n + r'_n\} \sim \{r + r'\}$, $\{r_n r'_n\} \sim \{rr'\}$. Hence, by Lemma 4, $r_n + r'_n \to r + r'$, $r_n r'_n \to rr'$.

● EXERCISES

1.* Let $\{r_n\} \sim \{r'_n\}$ and $\{r'_n\} \sim \{r''_n\}$. Prove that for each m there is an N such that for $n > N$ then $|r_n, r'_n| < 1/m$ and $|r'_n, r''_n| < 1/m$.

2.* Prove Lemma 5 above.

3. If $\{r_n\}$ is a Cauchy sequence and all r_n are in Z, what can you say about "most" of the r_n?

4. Prove that the two sequences $\{1 + 1/n\}$, $\{n/(n + 1)\}$ are equivalent. (Make sure that they are Cauchy first.) *Show conv. to same limit.*

5. Repeat exercise 4 for the sequences $\{1/n\}$, $\{1/n^2\}$. *by diff of 2 limits is 0 so N.S. so equiv.*

6. Are the sequences $\{2^n\}$, $\{2^n + 1/n\}$ equivalent?

7. Let $r'_n = r_n$ for $n \geq 1713$. Is $\{r'_n\} \sim \{r_n\}$ when $\{r_n\}$ is a Cauchy sequence? Can 1713 be replaced by any other number?

8. Suppose you know that $r_n \to 1/6$ and $r'_n \to 3$. What can you say about the limits of $r_n + r'_n$ and $r_n r'_n$?

9.* Give necessary and sufficient conditions that $\{r\} \sim \{r'\}$.

10. Deduce the results of exercise 7, p. 76, from the results of this section.

11. If $\{r_n\}$ and $\{r_n + r'_n\}$ are convergent, is $\{r'_n\}$ necessarily convergent? If so prove it—if not give a counter-example.

V The Nonnegative Real Numbers

V.1. Equivalence Classes Again

Let Q denote the collection of all Cauchy sequences of positive rational numbers. Thus the elements of Q are Cauchy sequences. Using the notion of equivalence of Cauchy sequences, defined in Section IV.7, we can split all of Q into equivalence classes. The set of all Cauchy sequences equivalent to a given Cauchy sequence constitutes an equivalence class.

We denote the collection of equivalence classes of Q by R^+. Elements of R^+ will, in general, be denoted by small Greek letters with or without subscripts. Thus if α and β are in R^+, they are equivalence classes of Cauchy sequences of Q.

LEMMA 1. *Given α, β then either α is identical with β (that is, $\alpha = \beta$) or α and β have no Cauchy sequences in common.*

Proof: If α and β are disjoint, there is nothing to prove. Hence, suppose $\{a_n\}$ is in both α and β. Then $\{a_n\} \sim \{a_n'\}$ and $\{a_n\} \sim \{b_n'\}$, where $\{a_n'\}$, $\{b_n'\}$ are the fixed sequences giving rise to α, β respectively. Hence, $\{a_n'\} \sim \{b_n'\}$. Thus, if $\{c_n\}$ is in α, then $\{c_n\} \sim \{a_n'\}$ and therefore $\{c_n\} \sim \{b_n'\}$, and $\{c_n\}$ is in β. Therefore, α is contained in β. Similarly, β is contained in α. Hence, $\alpha = \beta$.

Repetitious Remarks: (a) α in R^+ is made up of equivalent Cauchy sequences of Q;

(b) If α, β are in R^+ and $\alpha \neq \beta$, then α, β are disjoint;

(c) If $\{r_n\}$ is a Cauchy sequence, there is exactly one α in R^+ such that $\{r_n\}$ is in α;

(d) If $\{r_n\}$ and $\{r_n'\}$ are both in α, where α is in R^+, then $\{r_n\} \sim \{r_n'\}$.

(e) If $\{r_n\}$ is in α which is in R^+ and if $\{r'_n\} \sim \{r_n\}$, then $\{r'_n\}$ is in α.

(f) We shall, unless we state explicitly to the contrary, use small Greek letters for elements of R^+;

(g) R^+ is the collection of nonnegative real numbers. Throughout the rest of this chapter we shall use the phrase "real number" for "nonnegative real number."

V.2. Operations in R⁺

Let α and β be two real numbers. Then if $\{r_n\}$ and $\{\bar{r}_n\}$ are in α while $\{r'_n\}$ and $\{\bar{r}'_n\}$ are in β, then by Lemma 3, p. 77, the Cauchy sequences (see Lemma 2, p. 77) $\{r_n + r'_n\}$ and $\{\bar{r}_n + \bar{r}'_n\}$ are in the same element of R^+. Similarly, the Cauchy sequences $\{r_n r'_n\}$ and $\{\bar{r}_n \bar{r}'_n\}$ are in the same element of R^+.

These remarks justify the following definitions of addition $\oplus$ and multiplication $\odot$ in R^+.

$\alpha \oplus \beta$ is that element of R^+ containing $\{r_n + r'_n\}$, where $\{r_n\}$ is an arbitrary element of α and $\{r'_n\}$ is an arbitrary element of β.

$\alpha \odot \beta$ is that element of R^+ containing $\{r_n r'_n\}$, where $\{r_n\}$ is an arbitrary element of α and $\{r'_n\}$ is an arbitrary element of β.

Remarks: (a) Note that the operations $\oplus$, $\odot$ as defined here have nothing to do with the operations $\oplus$, $\odot$ as defined in Chapter III. No ambiguity should arise, since we no longer use $\oplus$, $\odot$ for the operations defined in Chapter III.

(b) After noting that the new $\oplus$, $\odot$ are not the same as the old $\oplus$, $\odot$ note how Lemma 3, p. 77, plays the role of the preliminary lemmas given in Sections III.2 and III.3. Without Lemma 3 here and the lemmas mentioned in Chapter III, none of the operations defined could have been defined in the way they were.

We shall use the symbol $\overline{\{r_n\}}$ for the equivalence class containing the Cauchy sequence $\{r_n\}$. Clearly, if $\{r_n\}$ is not a Cauchy sequence then $\overline{\{r_n\}}$ is not defined by the above. If $\{r_n\} \sim \{r'_n\}$, then $\overline{\{r_n\}} = \overline{\{r'_n\}}$ and conversely.

LEMMA 2. $\alpha \oplus \beta = \beta \oplus \alpha$, $\alpha \odot \beta = \beta \odot \alpha$.

Proof: Let $\alpha = \overline{\{a_n\}}$, $\beta = \overline{\{b_n\}}$. Then $\alpha \oplus \beta = \overline{\{a_n\}} \oplus \overline{\{b_n\}} = \overline{\{a_n + b_n\}} = \overline{\{b_n + a_n\}} = \overline{\{b_n\}} \oplus \overline{\{a_n\}} = \beta \oplus \alpha$. Similarly, $\alpha \odot \beta = \overline{\{r_n r_n'\}} = \overline{\{r_n' r_n\}} = \beta \odot \alpha$.

LEMMA 3. $\alpha \oplus (\beta \oplus \gamma) = (\alpha \oplus \beta) \oplus \gamma$, $\alpha \odot (\beta \odot \gamma) = (\alpha \odot \beta) \odot \gamma$.

Proof: Let $\alpha = \overline{\{a_n\}}$, $\beta = \overline{\{b_n\}}$, $\gamma = \overline{\{c_n\}}$. Then $\alpha \oplus (\beta \oplus \gamma) = \overline{\{a_n\}} \oplus (\overline{\{b_n\}} \oplus \overline{\{c_n\}}) = \overline{\{a_n\}} \oplus \overline{\{b_n + c_n\}} = \overline{\{a_n + (b_n + c_n)\}} = \overline{\{(a_n + b_n) + c_n\}} = \overline{\{a_n + b_n\}} \oplus \overline{\{c_n\}} = (\overline{\{a_n\}} \oplus \overline{\{b_n\}}) \oplus \overline{\{c_n\}} = (\alpha \oplus \beta) \oplus \gamma$.

The second half of this exercise is left for exercise 4, below.

LEMMA 4. $\alpha \odot (\beta \oplus \gamma) = (\alpha \odot \beta) \oplus (\alpha \odot \gamma)$.

Proof: Exercise 5, below.

The above definitions and lemmas give us the following information about the system $(R^+; \oplus, \odot)$.

  (i) it is closed with respect to $\oplus$, $\odot$;

  (ii) it is commutative with respect to $\oplus$, $\odot$;

  (iii) it is associative with respect to $\oplus$, $\odot$;

  (iv) $\odot$ is distributive over $\oplus$.

In the next section, we introduce a linear ordering relation $\oslash$. (This is not, of course, the same as the $\oslash$ defined in Chapter III.)

● **EXERCISES**

1. In the proof of Lemma 1 show that β is contained in α.

2. Prove remark (d), Section V.1.

3. Prove remark (e), Section V.1.

4. Complete the proof of Lemma 3.

5. Prove Lemma 4.

6.* Show that $\overline{\{1/n\}}$ satisfies the equation $x \oplus \beta = \beta$ for all β. This quantity $\overline{\{1/n\}}$ is thus the "additive identity" of $(R^+; \oplus, \odot)$.

7. Justify the use of the word "the" rather than "an" before "additive" in exercise 6.

8. Solve the equation $\overline{\{n/(n+1)\}} \oplus x = \overline{\{2n^2/(n^2+1)\}}$.

9. Solve the equation $\overline{\{1/n\}} \odot x = \overline{\{1/n\}}$. How many solutions are there?

10.* Can the equation $\overline{\{1/n\}} \odot x = \overline{\{1\}}$ be solved in R⁺? Explain your answer.

V.3. Linear Order Relation in R⁺

Let $\{a_n\}$, $\{b_n\}$ be two Cauchy sequences such that $a_n < b_n$ for all $n > N$. Then it is *not* necessary that there exist an integer m such that $a_n + 1/m < b_n$ for all $n > N$. For instance, if $a_n = 1/n$, $b_n = 2/n$, we have $a_n < b_n$ for all n, but $a_n + 1/m < b_n$ for all n is false no matter what m is taken to be. It is false, since its truth would imply $1/m < 1/n$ for all n, and this is false. However, there *may* exist an m such that $a_n + 1/m < b_n$ for $n > N$. We shall be quite interested in just such situations.

LEMMA 5. *If m is a fixed integer such that $a_n + 1/m < b_n$ for all $n > N$, and if $\{a_n'\} \sim \{a_n\}$, $\{b_n'\} \sim \{b_n\}$, then there is an N' such that $a_n + 1/(2m) < b_n'$ for all $n > N'$.*

Proof: By exercise 1, p. 79, there is an N_1 such that for $n > N_1$

$$|a_n, a_n'| < 1/(4m), \quad |b_n, b_n'| < 1/(4m). \tag{*}$$

Taking $N' = \max(N, N_1)$ we have for $n > N'$ the above two expressions and also $a_n + 1/m < b_n$. Now from (*) we have

$$a_n' < a_n + 1/(4m), \quad b_n < b_n' + 1/(4m)$$

for $n > N'$. These, along with $a_n + 1/m < b_n$, $n > N'$, yield

$$a_n' + 3/(4m) < a_n + 1/m < b_n < b_n' + 1/(4m),$$

and therefore $a_n' + 1/(2m) < b_n'$ for $n > N'$. This completes the proof.

The argument given in the proof of Lemma 5 might be clarified by considering the following, which applies for n sufficiently large.

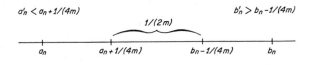

Hence, $a_n' + 1/(2m) < b_n'$.

We are now in a position to define the relation $\oslash$.

DEFINITION. *We say that $\alpha \otimes \beta$ if for some $\{a_n\}$ in α and some $\{b_n\}$ in β there are integers m and N such that $a_n + 1/m < b_n$ for $n > N$.*

Note that Lemma 5 assures us that if $\alpha \otimes \beta$, then it is not true that $\beta \otimes \alpha$. That is, the choice of $\{a_n\}$ in α and $\{b_n\}$ in β does not affect the $\otimes$ relation—if for one choice we get $\alpha \otimes \beta$ then we get $\alpha \otimes \beta$ for every choice. (Note, however, that an m which works for one choice need not work for another choice.)

We wish next to show that $\otimes$ is a linear ordering relation in $(R^+; \oplus, \odot)$.

LEMMA 6. $(R^+; \oplus, \odot; \otimes)$ *is linearly ordered with respect to $\otimes$.*

Proof: (a) Quite clearly there is no m such that $a_n + 1/m < a_n$ for all n sufficiently large. Hence, $\overline{\{a_n\}} \otimes \overline{\{a_n\}}$ is always false.

(b) Let $\alpha = \overline{\{a_n\}}$, $\beta = \overline{\{b_n\}}$, $\alpha \neq \beta$. We need to show that either $\alpha \otimes \beta$ or $\beta \otimes \alpha$. Since $\alpha \neq \beta$, we know $\{a_n\}$ is not equivalent to $\{b_n\}$. Thus, there exists an m such that no matter how large N may be there are integers $n > N$ such that $|a_n, b_n| > 1/m$. For such an m let N' be such that for $q > N'$, $n > N'$, we have

$$|a_n, a_q| < 1/(3m), \quad |b_n, b_q| < 1/(3m).$$

Now choose n such that $n > N'$ and $|a_n, b_n| > 1/m$. Then assuming (without loss of generality) that $a_n < b_n$ we have for $q > N'$ the situation expressed in the diagram below. Hence, $a_q + 1/(3m) < b_q$, and the proof of (b) is complete.

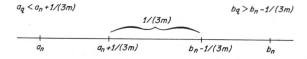

(c) Let $\alpha = \overline{\{a_n\}}$, $\beta = \overline{\{b_n\}}$, $\gamma = \overline{\{c_n\}}$, $\alpha \otimes \beta$, $\beta \otimes \gamma$. We are to show $\alpha \otimes \gamma$. Since $\alpha \otimes \beta$, there is an m' such that $a_n + 1/m' < b_n$ for all sufficiently large n. Since $\beta \otimes \gamma$, there is an m'' such that $b_n + 1/m'' < c_n$ for all sufficiently large n. Hence, for all n sufficiently large,

$$a_n + 1/m' + 1/m'' < b_n + 1/m'' < c_n.$$

Taking m such that $1/m < 1/m' + 1/m''$ yields the conclusion,

$$a_n + 1/m < c_n$$

for all sufficiently large n. This completes the proof.

if $x \neq 0$ *the* $x > 0$

LEMMA 7. *If* $\alpha \neq \overline{\{1/n\}}$, *then* $\overline{\{1/n\}} \bigotimes \alpha$.

Proof: Suppose for some α, $\alpha \bigotimes \overline{\{1/n\}}$. Let $\alpha = \overline{\{a_n\}}$. Then since $\{a_n\}$ is in α and $\{1/n\}$ is in $\overline{\{1/n\}}$, there must be an m such that $a_n + 1/m < 1/n$ for all n sufficiently large. But for $n > m$ we clearly have $\underline{a_n + 1/m} > 1/m > 1/n$. This is a contradiction. Therefore, $\alpha \bigotimes \{1/n\}$ is false, and the proof is complete.

COROLLARY. *Every Cauchy sequence which is not equivalent to* $\{1/n\}$ *has a lower bound.*

Proof: Let $\{a_n\}$ be a Cauchy sequence not equivalent to $\{1/n\}$. Then, by the lemma, $\overline{\{1/n\}} \bigotimes \overline{\{a_n\}}$, and therefore there is an m such that $1/n + 1/m < a_n$ for all $n > N$ for some N. Let $M = \min(a_1, \cdots, a_N, 1/m)$. Then $a_n \geq M$ for all n.

LEMMA 8. *If* $\{a_n\}$ *is a Cauchy sequence not equivalent to* $\{1/n\}$, *then* $\{1/a_n\}$ *is a Cauchy sequence.*

We can't prove this.
We prove if have
C.S. not N.S then
reciprocals.

Proof: We need to prove that, for fixed m,

$$\left| 1/a_n, 1/a_{n'} \right| < 1/m$$

for all sufficiently large n, n'. By the corollary to Lemma 7 there is an M such that $M < a_n$ for all n. Choose m' such that $m'M^2 > m$. Since $\{a_n\}$ is a Cauchy sequence, $\left| a_n, a_{n'} \right| < 1/m'$ for all sufficiently large n. Hence, by multiplying by $1/(a_n a_{n'})$ we have

$$\left| 1/a_{n'}, 1/a_n \right| < 1/(m' a_n a_{n'}) < 1/(m'M^2) < 1/m$$

for all sufficiently large n, n'. This completes the proof.

COROLLARY. *If* $\{a_n\}$, $\{b_n\}$ *are Cauchy sequences and* $\{b_n\}$ *is not equivalent to* $\{1/n\}$, *then* $\{a_n/b_n\}$ *is a Cauchy sequence.*

Proof: See exercise 1, p. 86.

LEMMA 9. *If* $\{a_n\}$, $\{b_n\}$ *are Cauchy sequences and* $a_n < b_n$ *for all* n, *then* $\{b_n - a_n\}$ *is a Cauchy sequence.*

Proof: Let m be a positive integer. Since $\{a_n\}$, $\{b_n\}$ are Cauchy sequences,

$$\left| a_{n'}, a_n \right| < 1/(2m)$$

and

$$\left| b_n, b_{n'} \right| < 1/(2m)$$

this is of no use to us.

for n, n' sufficiently large. Adding b_n and a_n respectively to these inequalities gives

$$\left| a_{n'} + b_n, a_n + b_n \right| < 1/(2m)$$

and

$$\left| b_n + a_n, b_{n'} + a_n \right| < 1/(2m).$$

Therefore, combining these we find

$$\left| a_{n'} + b_n, b_{n'} + a_n \right| < 1/m.$$

Finally, subtracting $a_n + a_{n'}$ gives

$$\left| b_n - a_n, b_{n'} - a_{n'} \right| < 1/m$$

for n, n' sufficiently large. This completes the proof.

● EXERCISES

1. Prove the corollary to Lemma 8.

2.* Solve the equation $\alpha \odot x = \beta$, where $\alpha \neq \overline{\{1/n\}}$. [*Hint:* Let $\alpha = \overline{\{a_n\}}$, $\beta = \overline{\{b_n\}}$ and consider the sequence $\{b_n/a_n\}$.]

3.* Prove that the solution in exercise 2 is unique. [*Hint:* Prove that if $\{a_n\}$ is a Cauchy sequence not equivalent to $\{1/n\}$ then $\{a_n x_n\} \sim \{a_n y_n\}$ implies that $\{x_n\} \sim \{y_n\}$.]

4. Let $\alpha = \overline{\{a_n\}}$, $\beta = \overline{\{b_n\}}$. Prove that when $\alpha \ominus \beta$ there exists a sequence $\{a_n'\}$ in α such that $a_n' < b_n$ for *all* n.

5.* Let $\alpha \ominus \beta$ or $\alpha = \beta$. Show that the equation $\alpha \oplus x = \beta$ has a solution in R^+. [*Hint:* Use problem 4 and Lemma 9.]

6.* Show that the solution in exercise 5 is unique. [*Hint:* Show that $\{a_n + x_n\} \sim \{a_n + y_n\}$ implies $\{x_n\} \sim \{y_n\}$.]

7.* Show that the equation $x^2 = \overline{\{2\}}$ is solvable in R^+. (Note that x^2 is to mean $x \odot x$.)

V.4. R^+ an Extension of R

We have seen that if r is any rational number, then the constant sequence $\{r\}$ is a Cauchy sequence. Hence, to each rational number r we can associate the element $\overline{\{r\}}$ of R^+. The totality of elements of R^+ thus singled out will be denoted by R_R^+. To state it another way, R_R^+ is the collection of elements of R^+ each of which contains a Cauchy sequence of the form $\{r\}$.

● EXAMPLES

(a) If $\alpha = \overline{\{1 + 1/n\}}$, then α is in R_R^+, since $\{1\}$ is in α. $\{1\}$ is in α, since $\{1\} \sim \{1 + 1/n\}$.

(b) If $\alpha = \overline{\{1/n\}}$, then α is not in R_R^+, since for no positive rational r do we have $\{r\} \sim \{1/n\}$.

(c) If $\alpha = \overline{\{r_n\}}$, where $r_n = 1 + q + q^2 + \cdots + q^n$, $q < 1$, then α is in R_R^+, since $\{1/(1 - q)\}$ is in α. This is true since [see example (d), p. 71], $r_n \to 1/(1 - q)$, and hence by Lemma 4, p. 78, $\{r_n\} \sim \{1/(1 - q)\}$.

(d) Let $r_n^2 \to 2$. Then $\alpha = \overline{\{r_n\}}$ is not in R_R^+, since if it were, then $\{r_n\} \sim \{r\}$ for some positive rational, r and hence by Lemma 4, p. 78, $r_n \to r$, which implies (see Lemma 4, p. 74) $r_n^2 \to r^2$, and this, by uniqueness of limits, means $r^2 = 2$, which contradicts exercise 2, p. 63.

THEOREM. $(R; +, \cdot\, ; <) \cong (R_R^+; +; \oplus, \odot\, ; \oslash)$;

Proof: We need to find a 1 to 1 mapping f of R onto R_R^+ such that

(i) $f(r_1 + r_2) = f(r_1) \oplus f(r_2)$;

(ii) $f(r_1 \cdot r_2) = f(r_1) \odot f(r_2)$;

(iii) $r_1 < r_2$ implies $f(r_1) \oslash f(r_2)$.

We take f to be the mapping $r \longleftrightarrow \overline{\{r\}}$. Thus, $f(r) = \overline{\{r\}}$. This mapping is clearly 1 to 1, since each r is mapped into something, every $\overline{\{r\}}$ has something mapped into it, and no two different r's, say r and r', get mapped into the same thing. (Note that for $r \neq r'$, $\overline{\{r\}} \neq \overline{\{r'\}}$. Proof of this is exercise 1, p. 88.)

(i) $f(r_1 + r_2) = \overline{\{r_1 + r_2\}} = \overline{\{r_1\}} \oplus \overline{\{r_2\}} = f(r_1) \oplus f(r_2)$, by definition of $\oplus$;

(ii) $f(r_1 \cdot r_2) = \overline{\{r_1 \cdot r_2\}} = \overline{\{r_1\}} \odot \overline{\{r_2\}} = f(r_1) \odot f(r_2)$, by definition of $\odot$;

(iii) if $r_1 < r_2$, then there is an m such that $r_1 + 1/m < r_2$. Hence, by definition of $\oslash$, $\overline{\{r_1\}} \oslash \overline{\{r_2\}}$. But this last is equivalent to $f(r_1) \oslash f(r_2)$. This completes the proof of the theorem.

Just as the elements of Z_R took on the names of their corresponding elements in Z the elements of R_{R+} take on the names of their corresponding elements in R. In this sense we say that R is contained in R⁺. Also, we write $+, \cdot, <$ instead of the more cumbersome $\oplus, \odot, \otimes$. No confusion should arise.

We now have the system $(R^+; +, \cdot; <)$, which satisfies the following properties.

(i) it is closed with respect to $+$ and $\cdot$;

(ii) it is commutative with respect to $+$ and $\cdot$;

(iii) it is associative with respect to $+$ and $\cdot$;

(iv) $\cdot$ is distributive over $+$;

(v) it is linearly ordered with respect to $<$;

(vi) there is an additive identity $\overline{\{1/n\}}$ which we shall denote by 0 (exercise 6, p. 000).

We shall prove many other familiar properties of the nonnegative real numbers in the following exercises. However, we shall not give an exhaustive treatment.

● EXERCISES

1.* Prove $\overline{\{r\}} = \overline{\{r'\}}$ if and only if $r = r'$.

2.* By exercises 2 and 3, p. 86, the equation $\alpha x = \beta$ has a unique solution when $\alpha \neq 0$. Denote the solution by β/α. By exercises 5 and 6, p. 86, the equation $\alpha + x = \beta$ has a unique solution when $\alpha < \beta$ or $\alpha = \beta$. Denote this solution by $\beta - \alpha$. Prove the following when both β and σ are different from 0.

(i) $\alpha/\beta + \gamma/\sigma = (\alpha\sigma + \beta\gamma)/\beta\sigma$;

(ii) $(\alpha/\beta)(\gamma/\sigma) = (\alpha\gamma)/(\beta\sigma)$;

(iii) $\alpha/\beta - \gamma/\sigma = (\alpha\sigma - \beta\gamma)/(\beta\sigma)$ when $\gamma/\sigma \leq \alpha/\beta$;

(iv) $\alpha/\beta < \gamma/\sigma$ when $\alpha\sigma < \beta\gamma$.

[*Hint:* Prove exercise 5(i) first, and make use of it for part (iii).]

3.* Prove that $(R_{R+}; +, \cdot; <)$ is an extension of $(Z; +, \cdot; <)$. Characterize the subset of R_{R+} which Z maps into. Denote it by Z_{R+}.

4.* Prove that if $\alpha \neq 0$, then for each β there is an element, say γ, in Z_{R+} such that $\beta < \gamma\alpha$ (Archimedean property). [*Hint:* Let $\beta = \overline{\{b_n\}}$, $\alpha = \overline{\{a_n\}}$. Then $\{b_n\}$ is bounded above, say by M, and $\{a_n\}$ is bounded below, say by A. Now choose n such that $nA > M + 1$, and take $\gamma = \overline{\{n\}}$. The conclusion follows.)

    5.* Let α, β, γ be in R$^+$, and suppose $\alpha < \beta$. Prove:

      (i) $\alpha\gamma < \beta\gamma$ for $\gamma \neq 0$;

      (ii) $\alpha + \gamma < \beta + \gamma$;

      (iii) $\alpha/\gamma < \beta/\gamma$ for $\gamma \neq 0$; *not true for us.*

      (iv) $1/\beta < 1/\alpha$ for $\alpha \neq 0$;

      (v) $\alpha < \alpha + \gamma$ for $\gamma \neq 0$;

      (vi) $\alpha < \beta + \gamma$;

     (vii) $\alpha/\beta < \overline{\{1\}}$; *not true for us*

    (viii) $\sqrt{\alpha} < \sqrt{\beta}$ (if both square roots exist);

      (ix) $\alpha^2 < \beta^2$;

      (x) $0 < \alpha$ for $\alpha \neq 0$. *not true for us*

    6. Prove that the equation $x^2 = \beta$ always is solvable in R$^+$ when β is in R_R+. (More is true, but we defer this until later.)

    7.* Repeat exercise 15, p. 54, when the R there is replaced by R$^+$.

V.5. The Fundamental Theorem

In this section, and only in this section, we shall *not* allow the elements of $R_R{}^+$ to take on the names of their correspondents in R. We first give a few definitions.

DEFINITION. *The symbol* $\left| \alpha, \beta \right| < \gamma$, *where* α, β, γ *are in* R$^+$, *means* $\alpha < \beta + \gamma$ *and* $\beta < \alpha + \gamma$.

This symbol enjoys the same properties that the corresponding symbol for rational numbers enjoys. In particular,

$$\left| \alpha, \beta \right| < \lambda \text{ and } \left| \beta, \gamma \right| < \lambda' \text{ imply } \left| \alpha, \gamma \right| < \lambda + \lambda'. \tag{*}$$

The proof of this is the same as that given for the rational number case. The properties given in exercises 3, 4, and 5, p. 70, carry over to the case where the a, b, c are real numbers rather than rational numbers.

Throughout the remainder of this section we use f to denote the isomorphism mapping introduced in the proof of the theorem in Section V.4.

DEFINITION. *The sequence* $\{\alpha_n\}$ *of real numbers* α_n *is said to* *converge to α, in symbols $\alpha_n \to \alpha$, if for each m there is an N such that*

$$|\alpha_n, \alpha| < f(1/m) \text{ for } n > N.$$

The sequence $\{\alpha_n\}$ of real numbers α_n is said to be a Cauchy sequence if for each m there is an N such that

$$|\alpha_q, \alpha_s| < f(1/m) \text{ for } q > N, s > N.$$

At this point we could prove many theorems about convergent sequences and Cauchy sequences of real numbers—theorems such as the following:

(1) If $\alpha_n \to \alpha$ and $\beta_n \to \beta$, then $a_n + \beta_n \to \alpha + \beta$ and $\alpha_n\beta_n \to \alpha\beta$.

(2) If $\{\alpha_n\}$ is a Cauchy sequence, then there is an M such that $\alpha_n < M$ for all n.

These theorems are easily proved, but we shall not carry out a general discussion of convergent and Cauchy sequences here. (Incidentally, the proofs of these two theorems are quite similar to the corresponding proofs for these theorems in R.) What we do wish to prove is a theorem whose analogue cannot be proved (since it is not true) in the rational numbers—namely:

THEOREM. *Every Cauchy sequence of real numbers converges to a real number.*

It is this theorem which embodies the truly fundamental difference between the rational numbers and the real numbers. Without this theorem the whole of the calculus as we know it would be drastically altered. Before proceeding to the proof of this theorem, we prove three lemmas which will be used in its proof.

LEMMA 1. R_{R^+} *is dense in* R^+. (*That is, between any two elements of R^+ there is an element of R_{R^+}.*)

Proof: Let $\alpha \neq \beta$. Then either $\alpha < \beta$ or $\beta < \alpha$. Without loss of generality, we suppose $\alpha < \beta$. Let $\alpha = \overline{\{a_n\}}$, $\beta = \overline{\{b_n\}}$. Then since $\alpha < \beta$, there is an m and an N such that

$$a_n + 1/m < b_n \text{ for } n > N.$$

Since $\{a_n\}$ is a Cauchy sequence, there is an N' such that

$$|a_q, a_s| < 1/(4m) \text{ for } q > N', s > N'.$$

Let $M = \max(N, N')$, and define c by the equation

$$c = a_{M+1} + 1/(2m)$$

We claim that $\alpha < f(c) < \beta$. Since $f(c)$ is in R_R^+, this will complete the proof. Before proving this, we wish to observe that since $M \geq N'$ we have

$$|a_{M+1}, a_n| < 1/(4m) \text{ for } n > M,$$

and hence

$$a_n < a_{M+1} + 1/(4m)$$

and

$$a_{M+1} < a_n + 1/(4m)$$

for $n > M$.

Now taking $m' = 4m$ we have

$$a_n + 1/m' = a_n + 1/(4m) < a_{M+1} + 1/(4m) + 1/(4m) = a_{M+1} + 1/(2m) = c \text{ for } n > M,$$

and

$$c + 1/m' = c + 1/(4m) = a_{M+1} + 3/(4m) < a_n + 1/(4m) + 3/(4m) = a_n + 1/m < b_n \text{ for } n > M.$$

Hence, by definition of $<$ we have

$$\alpha < f(c) < \beta,$$

and the proof is complete.

Remark: In the proof of Lemma 1 we have made use of the fact that the sequence $\{c\}$ is $f(c)$. That is, $f(c) = \{c\}$.

LEMMA 2. *The sequence $\{r_n\}$ is a Cauchy sequence if and only if the sequence $\{f(r_n)\}$ is a Cauchy sequence.*

Proof: The two sets of conditions

$$\begin{cases} r_s < r_q + 1/m \\ r_q < r_s + 1/m \end{cases}$$

and

$$\begin{cases} f(r_s) < f(r_q) + f(1/m) \\ f(r_q) < f(r_s) + f(1/m) \end{cases}$$

are equivalent because of the isomorphic character of f. Hence,

$$|r_q, r_s| < 1/m \text{ if and only if } |f(r_q), f(r_s)| < f(1/m).$$

This completes the proof.

Remarks: In the following lemma it is important to note that $f(c_n)$ is that real number which contains the *constant* sequence $\{c_n, c_n, c_n, \cdots\}$. Note that this constant sequence is *not* denoted by $\{c_n\}$. When we write $\{c_n\}$ we *always* mean $\{c_1, c_2, c_3, \cdots\}$. Similarly, $f(c_n + 1/m)$ is that real number which contains the constant sequence $\{c_n + 1/m, c_n + 1/m, c_n + 1/m, \cdots\}$. For each $f(c_n)$ the n is a fixed quantity.

LEMMA 3. *If $\{c_n\}$ is a Cauchy sequence, then $f(c_n) \to \overline{\{c_n\}}$.*

Proof: Let m' be an arbitrary integer. Since $\{c_n\}$ is a Cauchy sequence, there is an N such that $c_n < c_s + 1/(2m')$ and $c_s < c_n + 1/(2m')$ for $n > N$, $s > N$. Hence, for $n > N$, $s > N$,

$$c_n + 1/(4m') < c_s + 3/(4m') < c_s + 1/m'$$

and

$$c_s + 1/(4m') < c_n + 3/(4m') < c_n + 1/m'.$$

By the definition of $<$ these inequalities yield, respectively,

$$f(c_n) < \overline{\{c_n + 1/m'\}} = \overline{\{c_n\}} + f(1/m')$$

and

$$\overline{\{c_n\}} < f(c_n + 1/m') = f(c_n) + f(1/m').$$

Hence,

$$|f(c_n), \overline{\{c_n\}}| < f(1/m') \text{ for } n > N.$$

For each m' there is such an N, and therefore $f(c_n) \to \overline{\{c_n\}}$.

We are now prepared to prove the following theorem.

THEOREM. *Every Cauchy sequence of real numbers converges to a real number.*

Proof: Let $\{\alpha_n\}$ be a Cauchy sequence of real numbers. Then for each n, by Lemma 1, there is a rational number c_n such that

$$\alpha_n < f(c_n) < \alpha_n + f(1/n).$$

Thus

$$|\alpha_n, f(c_n)| < f(1/n) \text{ for all } n. \tag{**}$$

(a) We show first that $\{c_n\}$ is a Cauchy sequence. Let m be given. Since $\{\alpha_n\}$ is a Cauchy sequence, there is an N_1, such that

$$\left|\alpha_q, \alpha_s\right| < f(1/(3m)) \text{ for } q > N_1, s > N_1.$$

Let $N = \max(3m, N_1)$. Then

$$\left|\alpha_q, \alpha_s\right| < f(1/(3m)), \left|\alpha_q, f(c_q)\right| < f(1/q) < f(1/(3m)),$$

and

$$\left|\alpha_s, f(c_s)\right| < f(1/s) < f(1/(3m)) \text{ for } q > N \text{ and } s > N.$$

Hence, two application of (*), p. 89, yields

$$\left|f(c_q), f(c_s)\right| < f(1/m) \text{ for } q > N, s > N.$$

Since for each m we have such an N, $\{f(c_n)\}$ is a Cauchy sequence. Therefore by Lemma 2 above, $\{c_n\}$ is a Cauchy sequence.

(b) We show that $\alpha_n \to \overline{\{c_n\}}$. By Lemma 3 above, $f(c_n) \to \overline{\{c_n\}}$, so for each m there is an N_2 such that

$$\left|f(c_n), \overline{\{c_n\}}\right| < f(1/(2m)) \text{ for } n > N_2.$$

From (**) above,

$$\left|\alpha_n, f(c_n)\right| < f(1/(2m)) \text{ for } n > 2m.$$

Let $N = \max(N_2, 2m)$. Then an application of (*), p. 89, yields

$$\left|\alpha_n, \overline{\{c_n\}}\right| < f(1/m) \text{ for } n > N.$$

Thus, for each m such an N exists, and we conclude that $\alpha_n \to \overline{\{c_n\}}$. This completes the proof of the theorem.

● E X E R C I S E S

1. Prove (*), p. 89.

2. Why couldn't we prove that every Cauchy sequence of rational numbers converges to a rational number?

3. (a) Does every Cauchy sequence of elements of $R_R{}^+$ converge to an element in $R_R{}^+$?

(b) Does every Cauchy sequence of elements of $R_R{}^+$ converge to an element in R^+?

4. Prove that R^+ is dense with respect to $<$.

5. Give a proof that $f(r_n) \to f(r)$, when $r_n \to r$, without using either Lemma 2 or the main theorem. [*Hint:* A proof similar to the proof of Lemma 2 might work.]

6.* Prove $0 \cdot \alpha = 0$ for all α.

7. Let $\alpha_n = \overline{\{a_{n1}, a_{n2}, a_{n3}, \cdots\}}$ and suppose $\{\alpha_n\}$ is a Cauchy sequence. Show that $\{a_{11}, a_{22}, a_{33}, \cdots\}$ is not necessarily a Cauchy sequence.

8. Prove (1) and (2) on p. 90.

9. Prove $x^2 = \beta$ is solvable in R^+ for all β in R^+. (Compare with exercise 6, p. 89.)

From now on elements in R_{R^+} take on the names of their correspondents in R, and we shall use R for R_{R^+}. When we say "rational number" we shall mean "number in R_{R^+}."

VI The Real Numbers

VI.1. The Next Step

In this section all proofs are left to the reader, though occasional hints will be provided. Consider the Cartesian product $R^+ \times R^+$. This Cartesian product consists of all ordered pairs (a, b), where a, b are in R^+.

DEFINITION 1. *The pair (a, b) in $R^+ \times R^+$ is equivalent to the pair (c, d) in $R^+ \times R^+$, written $(a, b) \sim (c, d)$, if and only if $a + d = b + c$.*

Standard Remark: The use here of the word "equivalent" and of the symbol $\sim$ is, of course, not to be confused with earlier uses of the same word and symbol.

LEMMA 1.   (i) $(a, b) \sim (a, b)$;
          (ii) $(a, b) \sim (c, d)$ *if and only if* $(c, d) \sim (a, b)$;
         (iii) $(a, b) \sim (c, d)$ *and* $(c, d) \sim (e, f)$ *imply*
            $(a, b) \sim (e, f)$.

COROLLARY. $(a, b) \sim (e, f)$ *and* $(c, d) \sim (e, f)$ *imply* $(a, b) \sim (c, d)$.

DEFINITION 2. *An equivalence class of $R^+ \times R^+$ is a collection of all elements of $R^+ \times R^+$ each of which is equivalent to a given fixed element of $R^+ \times R^+$.*

LEMMA 2. *(a, b) and (c, d) are in the same equivalence class if and only if $(a, b) \sim (c, d)$.*

COROLLARY. *Two equivalence classes are identical or are disjoint.*

LEMMA 3. *If $(a, b) \sim (a', b')$ and $(c, d) \sim (c', d')$, then:*
(i) $(a + c, b + d) \sim (a' + c', b' + d')$;
(ii) $(ac + bd, ad + bc) \sim (a'c' + b'd', a'd' + b'c')$.

95

[*Hint:* To prove (ii), multiply the equation $a + b' = b + a'$ successively by c, d, getting two new equations. Similarly, multiply the equation $c + d' = c' + d$ successively by a', b', getting two more equations. The four equations thus obtained if added properly should yield (ii).]

We shall use the symbol $R^{\#}$ to denote the collection of equivalence classes of $R^+ \times R^+$. In general we shall use small Greek letters for elements of $R^{\#}$. If (a, b) is in α, then we shall use $\overline{(a, b)}$ as a name for α and write $\alpha = \overline{(a, b)}$. Hence, $\overline{(a, b)}$ is the equivalence class of $R^+ \times R^+$ containing (a, b). Elements of $R^{\#}$ are called *real numbers*.

DEFINITION 3.   *Let* $\alpha = \overline{(a, b)}$, $\beta = \overline{(c, d)}$. *Then define*

$$\alpha \oplus \beta = \overline{(a + c, b + d)},$$
$$\alpha \odot \beta = \overline{(ac + bd, ad + bc)}.$$

● E X E R C I S E. Show that the addition and multiplication of elements of $R^{\#}$ as given in Definition 3 are well defined. [*Hint:* Lemma 3 is the key.]

LEMMA 4.   (i) $\alpha \oplus \beta = \beta \oplus \alpha$; $\alpha \odot \beta = \beta \odot \alpha$;
        (ii) $(\alpha \oplus \beta) \oplus \gamma = \alpha \oplus (\beta \oplus \gamma)$; $(\alpha \odot \beta) \odot \gamma = \alpha \odot (\beta \odot \gamma)$;
        (iii) $\alpha \odot (\beta \oplus \gamma) = (\alpha \odot \beta) \oplus (\alpha \odot \gamma)$.

DEFINITION 4. $\bar{0} = \overline{(0, 0)}$, $\bar{1} = \overline{(1, 0)}$.

LEMMA 5.   (i) $\overline{(a, a)} = \bar{0}$;
        (ii) $\overline{(a + b, c + b)} = \overline{(a, c)}$.

LEMMA 6.   *Every element of* $R^{\#}$ *can be written in the form* $\overline{(a, b)}$, *where one or both of a, b is 0.* [*Hint:* $\overline{(c, d)}$ is equal to $\overline{(0, 0)}$, $\overline{(c - d, 0)}$, $\overline{(0, d - c)}$ in the cases $c = d$, $c > d$, $c < d$, respectively.]

LEMMA 7.   (i) $\alpha \oplus x = \bar{0}$ *has a solution for each α*;
 (ii) $\alpha \oplus x = \beta$ *has a unique solution for each pair, α, β*;
(iii) $\alpha \odot x = \bar{1}$ *has a solution for each $\alpha \neq \bar{0}$*;
(iv) $\alpha \odot x = \beta$ *has a unique solution for each pair α, β, $\alpha \neq \bar{0}$.*
[*Hint:* In (i) try $x = \overline{(b, a)}$ when $\alpha = \overline{(a, b)}$.]

COROLLARY.   (i) $\alpha \oplus x = \bar{0}$ *has a unique solution;*
(ii) $\alpha \odot x = \bar{1}$ *has a unique solution for $\alpha \neq 0$.*

LEMMA 8. (i) $\alpha \oplus \beta = \alpha$ *for all* α *if and only if* $\beta = \bar{0}$;
(ii) $\alpha \odot \beta = \alpha$ *for all* α *if and only if* $\beta = \bar{1}$.

DEFINITION 5. (i) *Denote the unique solution of* $\alpha \oplus x = \beta$ *by* $\beta - \alpha$. *If* $\beta = \bar{0}$, *denote* $\beta - \alpha$ *by* $-\alpha$.
(ii) *Denote the unique solution of* $\alpha \odot x = \beta$, $\alpha \neq \bar{0}$, *by* β/α.

Remarks. (a) For each α there is a unique $-\alpha$ such that $\alpha \oplus (-\alpha) = \bar{0}$.
(b) For each $\alpha \neq \bar{0}$ there is a unique $\bar{1}/\alpha$ such that $\alpha \odot (\bar{1}/\alpha) = \bar{1}$.

LEMMA 9. (i) *If* $\alpha = \overline{(a, b)}$, *then* $-\alpha = \overline{(b, a)}$;
(ii) $-(-\alpha) = \alpha$;
(iii) $-(\alpha \oplus \beta) = (-\alpha) \oplus (-\beta)$. [*We shall use* $-\alpha - \beta$ for this right side.]

LEMMA 10. *If* $(a, b) \sim (c, d)$ *and* $a < b$, *then* $c < d$.

DEFINITION 6. *Elements of the form* $\overline{(a, 0)}$ *are called positive when* $a \neq 0$. *Those of the form* $\overline{(0, a)}$ *are called negative when* $a \neq 0$.

DEFINITION 7. (i) *Let* $\alpha = \overline{(a, b)}$, $\beta = \overline{(c, d)}$. *Then we shall say that* $\alpha \otimes \beta$ *when* $a + d < b + c$.
(ii) *If* $\alpha \otimes \beta$ *or* $\alpha = \beta$, *we shall write* $\alpha \otimes \beta$.

● E X E R C I S E . (a) Show that the relation $\otimes$ is well defined. That is, show that if $(a, b) \sim (a', b')$ and $(c, d) \sim (c', d')$, then $a + d < b + c$ implies $a' + d' < b' + c'$.
(b) Prove $\alpha \otimes \beta$ if and only if $-\alpha \oplus \beta$ is positive.

LEMMA 11. (i) α *is positive if and only if* $\bar{0} \otimes \alpha$;
(ii) α *is negative if and only if* $\alpha \otimes \bar{0}$;
(iii) α *is positive if and only if* $-\alpha$ *is negative*.

LEMMA 12. (i) *For no* α *do we have* $\alpha \otimes \alpha$.
(ii) *If* $\alpha \neq \beta$, *then* $\alpha \otimes \beta$ *or* $\beta \otimes \alpha$.
(iii) *If* $\alpha \otimes \beta$ *and* $\beta \otimes \gamma$, *then* $\alpha \otimes \gamma$.

LEMMA 13. (i) *If* $\alpha \otimes \beta$ *then* $\alpha \oplus \gamma \otimes \beta \oplus \gamma$.
(ii) *If* $\alpha \otimes \beta$ *and* $\bar{0} \otimes \gamma$ *then* $\alpha \odot \gamma \otimes \beta \odot \gamma$.

DEFINITION 8. $|\alpha| = \begin{cases} \alpha \text{ if } \bar{0} \otimes \alpha, \\ -\alpha \text{ if } \alpha \otimes \bar{0}. \end{cases}$

LEMMA 14.   (i) $|\alpha| \oslash \bar{0}$ for $\alpha \neq \bar{0}$;

(ii) $|\bar{0}| = \bar{0}$;

(iii) $|\alpha \odot \beta| = |\alpha| \odot |\beta|$;

(iv) $\alpha \oslash |\alpha|$, $-\alpha \oslash |\alpha|$,

(v) $|\alpha \oplus \beta| \oslash |\alpha| \oplus |\beta|$.

[*Hint:* In (v) we must have $|\alpha \oplus \beta|$ equal to $\alpha \oplus \beta$ or to $-(\alpha \oplus \beta)$. But by (iv) $\alpha \oplus \beta \oslash |\alpha| \oplus |\beta|$ and $-(\alpha \oplus \beta) = (-\alpha) \oplus (-\beta) \oslash |\alpha| \oplus |\beta|$.]

LEMMA 15. $(\mathrm{R}^{\#}; \oplus, \odot ; \oslash)$ *is an extension of* $(\mathrm{R}^{+}; +, \cdot ; <)$. [*Hint:* Consider the mapping f which takes a in R^{+} into $\overline{(a, 0)}$; that is, $f(a) = \overline{(a, 0)}$.]

LEMMA 16. $(\mathrm{R}^{\#}; \oplus, \odot ; \oslash)$ *is Archimedean.* [That is, given $\alpha \oslash 0$, $\beta \oslash 0$ there is a $\gamma = \overline{(n, 0)}$ such that $\gamma \odot \beta \oslash \alpha$.] [*Hint:* Write $\alpha = \overline{(a, 0)}$, $\beta = \overline{(b, 0)}$. Then $\gamma \odot \beta = \overline{(nb, 0)} \oslash \alpha$ for n sufficiently large.]

From the above properties of $(\mathrm{R}^{\#}; \oplus, \odot ; \oslash)$ we can derive *all* of the well known arithmetic properties. We do not carry out this task here.

VI.2. The System $(\mathbf{R}^{\#}; +, \cdot ; <)$

We now drop the circles around $+, \cdot, <$ and the bars over 0, 1. Also, we introduce the name $a - b$ for $\alpha = \overline{(a, b)}$. When $a \geq b$ we see that $a - b$ is defined in R^{+} and is the number corresponding to α. When $a < b$, $a - b$ is not defined in R^{+}, but is here defined to be the number $\overline{(a, b)}$ in $\mathrm{R}^{\#}$. [This convention is also in accord with the fact that if $\bar{a}$ and $\bar{b}$ are the images of a and b under f, then $\bar{a} + (\bar{b}-) = \overline{(a, b)}$.] If α in $\mathrm{R}^{\#}$ corresponds to a rational number or an integer via the chain of extensions $\mathrm{Z} \longleftrightarrow \mathrm{R} \longleftrightarrow \mathrm{R}^{+} \longleftrightarrow \mathrm{R}^{\#}$, then we say that α *and* $-\alpha$ are rational numbers or integers, respectively. Also, 0 is counted as an integer and as a rational number. Thus, the integers are now the elements of $\mathrm{R}^{\#}$ whose names are

$$\cdots, -5, -4, -3, -2, -1, 0, 1, 2, 3, 4, 5, \cdots.$$

The rational numbers are numbers which can be written in the form p/q, where p and q are integers with $q \neq 0$.

● E X A M P L E S. $-2 = \overline{(0,\,2)} = \overline{(5,\,7)} = \overline{(13,\,15)}$, $13 = \overline{(13,\,0)} = \overline{(14,\,1)} = \overline{(55/2,\,29/2)}$, $3/2 = \overline{(3/2,\,0)}$ $= \overline{(10,\,17/2)} = \overline{(3,\,3/2)}$, $-(17/23) = \overline{(0,\,17/23)}$.

Concerning the symbol $|\alpha,\beta| < \gamma$, we have the following lemma.

LEMMA. $|\alpha,\beta| < \gamma$ *if and only if* $|\alpha - \beta| < \gamma$.

Proof: We first note that neither $|\alpha,\beta| < \gamma$, $|\alpha - \beta| < \gamma$ is true unless $\gamma > 0$. We therefore assume that $\gamma > 0$.

(a) Suppose $|\alpha,\beta| < \gamma$. Then $\alpha < \beta + \gamma$ and $\beta < \alpha + \gamma$. This means $\alpha - \beta < \gamma$ and $\beta - \alpha < \gamma$. Since $|\alpha - \beta| = \alpha - \beta$ or $\beta - \alpha$, we conclude that $|\alpha - \beta| < \gamma$.

(b) Suppose $|\alpha - \beta| < \gamma$. Then $\alpha - \beta < \gamma$ and $-(\alpha - \beta) = \beta - \alpha < \gamma$. From this, $\alpha < \beta + \gamma$ and $\beta < \alpha + \gamma$, and therefore $|\alpha,\beta| < \gamma$.

Because of this lemma we will, henceforth, write $|\alpha - \beta| < \gamma$ in place of $|\alpha,\beta| < \gamma$. The earlier theorem

$$|\alpha,\beta| < \lambda,\ |\beta,\gamma| < \lambda' \text{ implies } |\alpha,\gamma| < \lambda + \lambda'$$

is now replaced by $|\alpha - \gamma| \le |\alpha - \beta| + |\beta - \gamma|$. The proof follows from Lemma 14 (v), p. 98 since by that result

$$|\alpha - \gamma| = |(\alpha - \beta) + (\beta - \gamma)| \le |\alpha - \beta| + |\beta - \gamma|.$$

We define Cauchy sequence and convergent sequence in a similar way to that done earlier in R and R⁺.

(i) $\{\alpha_n\}$ is a Cauchy sequence if for each $\epsilon > 0$ there is an N such that $|\alpha_q - \alpha_s| < \epsilon$ for $q > N$, $s > N$.

(ii) $\{\alpha_n\}$ is a convergent sequence, and converges to α, if for each $\epsilon > 0$ there is an N such that $|\alpha_q - \alpha| < \epsilon$ for $q > N$.

Remark: Since for each $\epsilon > 0$ there is an m such that $1/m < \epsilon$, these definitions are equivalent to those used earlier with $1/m$ instead of ϵ. Note, however, that our ϵ need not be the reciprocal of an integer.

LEMMA. *The sequence* $\{a_n\}$ *in* R⁺ *is a Cauchy sequence if and only if* $\{f(a_n)\}$ *in* R# *is a Cauchy sequence.* (The f here is the mapping of Lemma 15, p. 98.) The proof follows the same lines as the proof of Lemma 2, p. 91.

If $\{\alpha_n\}$ is a Cauchy sequence in R# and if $\alpha_n \ge 0$ for all n, then we can write $\alpha_n = \overline{(a_n, 0)}$ and by the preceding lemma $\{a_n\}$ is a Cauchy sequence in R^+. Now, by the last theorem in Chapter V, there is an a such that $a_n \rightarrow a$. We claim that $\alpha_n \rightarrow \overline{(a, 0)}$. This is true since

$$\left| \alpha_n - \overline{(a, 0)} \right| = \left| \overline{(a_n, 0)} - \overline{(a, 0)} \right| = \left| \overline{(a_n, a)} \right|$$

$$= \begin{cases} \overline{(a_n, a)} \text{ for } \overline{(a_n, a)} \geq 0, \\ \overline{(a, a_n)} \text{ for } \overline{(a_n, a)} < 0, \end{cases}$$

and both of these can be made less than ϵ for n sufficiently large, since $a_n \rightarrow a$. If α_n is not greater than or equal to 0 for all n, we can consider $\{\alpha_n + \beta\}$, where β is large enough so that $\alpha_n + \beta \geq 0$ for all n. Such a β exists, since, as usual, a Cauchy sequence is bounded (even below, since we now have negative numbers). Now $\{\alpha_n + \beta\}$ will converge by the above argument, and so there is a γ such that $\alpha_n + \beta \rightarrow \gamma$. It is not difficult to see that $\alpha_n \rightarrow \gamma - \beta$. Combining these remarks gives the following theorem.

THEOREM. *Every Cauchy sequence of numbers in $R^\#$ converges to a number in $R^\#$.*

VI.3. Least Upper Bounds

In this section we prove an important consequence of the theorem that every Cauchy sequence of real numbers converges. We first introduce some definitions.

DEFINITION. *An upper bound of a set of numbers is called a least upper bound (lub) if it is smaller than all other upper bounds of the set.*

Our first lemma asserts that if a set has a least upper bound, then it has only one.

LEMMA. *A set of numbers has at most one lub.*

Proof: See exercise 1, p. 103.

A similar definition and lemma apply to *greatest lower bound* (glb). (See exercise 2, p. 103.)

We shall sometimes denote the lub of a set S by lub S. Similarly, glb S designates the glb of S.

We now state and prove the main theorem of this section.

THEOREM 1. *Every set of real numbers which has an upper bound has a real number least upper bound.*

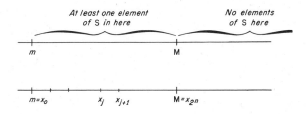

Remark. Note that if "real" is replaced by "rational," this theorem becomes false. The reader should supply an example illustrating this.

Proof: Let S be a set of numbers in $R^\#$ with an upper bound. Let M be an integer upper bound of S and let m be an integer which is smaller than at least one element of S. For each integer n divide the interval from m to M into 2^n equal subintervals by choosing $x_0, \cdots, x_{2^n}$ such that $x_j = j(M - m)/2^n + m$. Since at least one element of S lies between m and M there is a smallest x_j greater than all elements of S. Let this be x_{j_n}. Thus, for each n we have determined a number x_{j_n}. By construction we must have

$$x_{j_1} \geq x_{j_2} \geq x_{j_3} \geq \cdots$$

and

$$x_{j_{n-1}} < x_{j_{n+1}} \leq x_{j_n} \text{ for all } n.$$

Hence,

$$x_{j_n} - x_{j_{n+1}} < \frac{M - m}{2^n},$$

and therefore, when $n < q$,

$$\begin{aligned}
x_{j_n} - x_{j_q} &= x_{j_n} - x_{j_{n+1}} + x_{j_{n+1}} - x_{j_{n+2}} + \cdots + x_{j_{q-1}} - x_{j_q} \\
&< (M - m)(1/2^n + 1/2^{n+1} + \cdots + 1/2^{q-1}) \\
&< (1/2^{n-1})(M - m).
\end{aligned}$$

This means that $x_{j_1}, x_{j_2}, x_{j_3}, \cdots$ is a monotone decreasing Cauchy sequence. Thus, by the theorem on p. 100 the sequence converges, say to α. We claim that $\alpha = $ lub S. Certainly no element of S is greater than α, for if it were, then the decreasing sequence x_{j_n} of upper bounds of S would each have to be greater than this element, and the sequence could not tend to α. On the other hand, suppose there is an upper bound $\beta < \alpha$. Then each nonupper bound $x_{j_{n-1}}$ is $\leq \beta$. Since $x_{j_n} - x_{j_{n-1}} = (M - m)/2^n$ can be made smaller than $\alpha - \beta$ for n large enough, this would imply $x_{j_n} < \alpha$ for such n. But each x_{j_n} is $\geq \alpha$. Therefore, no such β exists, and the theorem is completely proved.

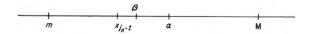

Sometimes Theorem 1 is taken as one of the axioms characterizing the real number system. We show how easily the fundamental theorem can be proved from this and the other axioms.

THEOREM 2. *Theorem 1 implies that every Cauchy sequence of real numbers converges.*

Proof: Let $\{\alpha_n\}$ be a Cauchy sequence and suppose M is an upper bound for the sequence. Define S to be the set of all numbers which are smaller than infinitely many α_n. (S is not empty, since $\{\alpha_n\}$, being Cauchy, has a lower bound.) Also, M is an upper bound

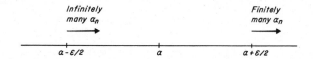

of S. Hence, S has a lub. Let $\alpha = \text{lub S}$. We claim that $\alpha_n \to \alpha$. Let $\epsilon > 0$ be given. By definition of α there are infinitely many n such that $\alpha - \epsilon/2 < \alpha_n$, but only finitely many n such that $\alpha + \epsilon/2 < \alpha_n$. Let N_1 be such that for $n > N_1$, $\alpha_n < \alpha + \epsilon/2$, and let N_2 be such that for $r > N_2$, $s > N_2$, then $|\alpha_r - \alpha_s| < \epsilon/2$. Define $N = \max(N_1, N_2)$ and let $t > N$ such that $\alpha - \epsilon/2 < \alpha_t$. Then $\alpha - \epsilon/2 < \alpha_t < \alpha + \epsilon/2$. Finally, we have for $n > N$

$$|\alpha - \alpha_n| = |\alpha - \alpha_t + \alpha_t - \alpha_n|$$
$$\leq |\alpha - \alpha_t| + |\alpha_t - \alpha_n| < \epsilon/2 + \epsilon/2 = \epsilon.$$

This completes the proof of the theorem.

The last theorem of Section VI.2 together with the first theorem of this section may be combined in the following theorem.

THEOREM 3. *Every Cauchy sequence of real numbers converges, and every set of real numbers with an upper bound has a least upper bound.*

● EXERCISES

1. Prove the first lemma of Section VI.3.

2. Give a definition of glb and prove the analogue of the first lemma of Section VI.3 for glb's.

3. Prove that every Cauchy sequence of real numbers is bounded.

4. Prove the following theorem.

If S is a set of real numbers with a lower bound, then S has a glb. [*Hint:* Define $\bar{S}$ to be the set of negatives of elements of S. Now $\bar{S}$ has an upper bound and therefore a lub. Let $\alpha = \text{lub } \bar{S}$. Prove glb $S = -\alpha$.]

5.* Prove the following theorems.

(a) If $\alpha_1 \leq \alpha_2 \leq \alpha_3 \leq \cdots$ and if there is an M such that $\alpha_n < M$ for all n, then the sequence $\{\alpha_n\}$ converges.

(b) If in (a) we also have $\gamma < \alpha_n \leq \beta$ for all n, then the limit, say α, of the sequence $\{\alpha_n\}$ satisfies $\gamma < \alpha \leq \beta$.

6. Rephrase exercise 5 for decreasing sequences.

7. Prove $|\alpha + \beta| \geq ||\alpha| - |\beta||$.

8.* Making use of the Archimedean property for $R^{\#}$ (see Lemma 16, p. 98) show that if $\alpha > 0$, $\beta > 0$, there is a greatest integer n such that $n\alpha < \beta$. (When $\beta < \alpha$ this greatest integer is 0.)

9.* Prove that if the sequence $\{\alpha_n\}$ converges and the subsequence $\{\alpha_{n_j}\}$ converges to α, then the sequence $\{\alpha_n\}$ converges to α.

10. A *Dedekind cut* in $R^{\#}$ is a splitting of all of $R^{\#}$ into two disjoint nonempty sets, say L and R, such that every element in L is less than every element in R. We denote a cut with sets L and R by [L, R]. Prove that either L has a greatest or R a least element but not both. Define a Dedekind cut in the rational numbers, and again consider this proposition.

VI.4. Base 10 Representation of Integers

Before proceeding to our main discussion we shall restate Lemma 1, p. 35, in a more convenient form. This was not possible in Chapter II, since there we did not have zero.

LEMMA 1. *If a and b are integers and a > 0, there exist unique integers q and r such that*

$$b = qa + r, \qquad 0 \le r < a.$$

Proof: See exercise 1, p. 105.

We shall make use of this lemma in the proof of the next theorem, which demonstrates the existence of the usual *base 10 representation* for the integers.

THEOREM. *Each nonnegative integer n can be written uniquely in the form*

$$n = a_s 10^s + a_{s-1} 10^{s-1} + \cdots + a_1 10 + a_0,$$

where $0 \le a_i < 10$ for each i, and $a_s \ne 0$.

Proof: The proof is by induction.

(i) For $n = 1$ we clearly must have $s = 0$ and $a_0 = 1$.

(ii) Suppose the theorem is true for $n \le m$. By the lemma there exist integers q and r such that

$$m + 1 = 10q + r, \qquad 0 \le r < 10.$$

By the induction hypothesis, since $q < m$,

$$q = b_t 10^t + \cdots + b_0, \qquad 0 \le b_i < 10, \qquad b_t \ne 0.$$

Hence,

$$m + 1 = b_t 10^{t+1} + \cdots + b_0 10 + r$$

Taking $s = t + 1$, $a_s = b_t$, $\cdots$, $a_1 = b_0$, $a_0 = r$ proves the existence of the representation for $m + 1$. Suppose now that there are two representations:

$$m + 1 = a_s 10^s + \cdots + a_1 10 + a_0 = c_v 10^v + \cdots + c_1 10 + c_0.$$

Then, by Lemma 2, p. 35, 10 divides $a_0 - c_0$. But since both a_0 and c_0 are between 0 and 9 inclusive, we must have $a_0 = c_0$. Hence,

$$(m + 1 - a_0)/10 = a_s 10^{s-1} + \cdots + a_1 = c_v 10_{v-1} + \cdots + c_1.$$

By the induction assumption, since $(m + 1 - a_0)/10 < m$, the representation for $(m + 1 - a_0)/10$ is unique, so $s = v$ and $a_s = c_s, \cdots,$ $a_1 = c_1$. This proves that the representation for $m + 1$ is unique and completes the induction and proof of the theorem.

This theorem is the real reason for using the particular names given to the natural numbers in Chapter II. The integer 143, for example, is that natural number whose representation as given by the above theorem is

$$1 \cdot 10^2 + 4 \cdot 10 + 3.$$

The name of the integer is merely the string of coefficients in its base 10 representation. (Of course zero and the first nine natural numbers must have been named first in order for this scheme to work.)

At this stage we can reflect upon Chapter II and realize that if there we had given the natural numbers some set of names that did not (in some way) presuppose this last theorem, then this theorem would seem to have more content. The fact that we have already used the names the theorem gives makes the theorem seem to say less than it actually does.

The theorems in the next section are of similar character but may appear somewhat more exciting. In that section we introduce for the real numbers representations which have not been previously used in this book. These representations lead to the usual "infinite decimals." Here too the edge may have been taken off, since everyone is familiar with infinite decimals even though they may never have seen a logical development of the correspondence between them and the real numbers.

Since we already have the usual representations for the integers, we may confine our attention in the next section to real numbers between 0 and 1 inclusive.

● EXERCISES

1.* Prove Lemma 1, p. 104.

2. (a) Let k be an integer greater than or equal to 2. Replace 10 in the theorem by k, and prove the new statement. (The result gives rise to the *base k* representation of the integers.)

(b) Write the base 2 and the base 7 representations of the integers 17, 101, 150.

3.* (a) Let α be a real number. Prove that the largest integer a that is less than or equal to α is determined by the inequalities

$$a \leq \alpha < a + 1.$$

(b) Conclude that if a and b are integers and $a \leq \alpha < a + 1$, $b \leq \alpha < b + 1$, then $a = b$.

4. Suppose $c_s 10^s + c_{s-1} 10^{s-1} + \cdots + c_1 10 + c_0 = 0$ and for all i, $-9 \leq c_i \leq 9$. Prove that $c_0 = c_1 = \cdots = c_s = 0$.

VI.5. Decimals

In the following discussion we do not need any prior knowledge of decimals. However, to gain a greater comprehension, the reader should try to interpret what is said in the light of his previous understanding of decimals.

LEMMA 1. *Let $a_1, a_2, \cdots$ be an arbitrary sequence of nonnegative integers all less than or equal to 9. Define*

$$s_n = a_1 10^{-1} + a_2 10^{-2} + \cdots + a_n 10^{-n}.$$

Then $s_n \to \alpha$ for some real number α, $0 \leq \alpha \leq 1$.

Proof: Since $s_{n+1} = s_n + a_{n+1} 10^{-n-1}$ and $a_{n+1} \geq 0$, we see that $s_n \leq s_{n+1}$ for all $n \geq 1$. Also, for $n \geq 1$, since each $a_i \leq 9$ we have

$$s_n \leq (9/10)(1 + 10^{-1} + \cdots + 10^{-n+1}) = 1 - 10^{-n} < 1.$$

(At the equality we used exercise 16, p. 54, with $q = 10^{-1}$.) Therefore, $\{s_n\}$ is an increasing sequence of nonnegative numbers with an upper bound of 1. By exercise 5, p. 103, we conclude that $s_n \to \alpha$ for some α, $0 \leq \alpha \leq 1$. This completes the proof.

When, as in the above lemma,

$$a_1 10^{-1} + a_2 10^{-2} + \cdots + a_n 10^{-n} \to \alpha$$

we shall write

$$\alpha = . \, a_1 a_2 \cdots$$

and call the right side an *infinite decimal* (or just a *decimal*). An infinite decimal is said to be *terminating* if it ends in all zeros, that is, if there is an N such that $a_n = 0$ for $n > N$. Otherwise it is called *nonterminating*. The a_i will be called the *digits* of the decimal. If in a terminating decimal $a_n = 0$, for $n > N$, then we write the decimal

$$. a_1 a_2 \cdots a_N.$$

● EXAMPLES

(a) Let $a_1 = 4$, $a_i = 9$ for $i > 1$. Then

$$s_n = 4/10 + 9/10^2 + 9/10^3 + \cdots + 9/10^n,$$

and (again using exercise 16, p. 54) $s_n \to 1/2$.

(b) Let $a_1 = 5$, $a_i = 0$ for $i > 1$. Then

$$s_n = 5/10 + 0/10^2 + \cdots + 0/10^n,$$

and $s_n \to 1/2$.

Hence, the nonterminating decimal

$$.4999 \cdots$$

and the terminating decimal

$$.5000 \cdots (= .5)$$

are both equal to $1/2$.

The above lemma does not guarantee that every real number α, $0 \leq \alpha \leq 1$, has an infinite decimal. The next lemma, however, assures us that this is the case.

LEMMA 2. *Let α be a real number $0 \leq \alpha \leq 1$. Then there exists a sequence of nonnegative integers $a_1, a_2, \cdots$ all less than or equal to 9 such that $\alpha = .a_1 a_2 \cdots$.*

Proof: For $\alpha = 1$ we take all $a_i = 9$. For other α we define the a_i recursively by

$$a_1 \leq 10\alpha < a_1 + 1;$$
$$a_n \leq 10^n(\alpha - a_1 10^{-1} - a_2 10^{-2} - \cdots - a_{n-1} 10^{-n+1}) < a_n + 1.$$

(These do define the a_n, as we have seen in exercise 3, p. 105.) To show that $s_n = a_1 10^{-1} + a_2 10^{-2} + \cdots + a_n 10^{-n} \to \alpha$, we merely multiply the second inequality through by 10^{-n} and then subtract $a_n 10^{-n}$ from all parts. This gives

$$0 \leq \alpha - s_n < 10^{-n}.$$

Since $10^{-n} \to 0$, we must have $\alpha - s_n \to 0$ and $s_n \to \alpha$, which proves the lemma.

There is one trouble with Lemma 2. It reads "there exists a sequence . . ." rather than "there exists a unique sequence . . . ." If we could strengthen Lemma 2 by inserting the word "unique," we could then say that Lemmas 1 and 2 together exhibit a 1 to 1 mapping between the set of all real numbers $0 \leq \alpha \leq 1$ and the set of all infinite sequences $a_1, a_2, \cdots, 0 \leq a_i \leq 9$.

Unfortunately, the lemma cannot be so strengthened. The strong form of the lemma is not true. However, as we shall see, the situation is not really so bad after all. "Usually" a real number α has a unique decimal expansion and when it does not it has only two such expansions, each of which is readily deduced from the other. Further, every real number *does* have a unique nonterminating decimal expansion.

The following two lemmas along with one of the exercises prove these assertions.

LEMMA 3. *Let* $\alpha = .a_1a_2 \cdots$, *where the decimal is not terminating and also does not end in all nines. Then no other decimal is equal to* α.

Proof: Let $\beta = .b_1b_2 \cdots$, where this decimal does not have the same digits as does $.a_1a_2 \cdots$. We show $\alpha \neq \beta$. Let q be the smallest subscript with $a_q \neq b_q$. Without loss of generality (Is this really true? See exercise 5, p. 111.), suppose $b_q < a_q$. Further, since the decimal $.a_1a_2 \cdots$ is not terminating, there is a smallest $s > q$ for which $a_s - b_s \neq -9$. Now,

$$a_i - b_i \geq -9 \text{ for all } i;$$
$$a_s - b_s \geq -8;$$
$$a_q - b_q \geq 1.$$

Hence, setting

$$s_n = a_1 10^{-1} + a_2 10^{-2} + \cdots + a_n 10^{-n};$$
$$s_n' = b_1 10^{-1} + b_2 10^{-2} + \cdots + b_n 10^{-n}$$

we have, for $n > s$,

$$\begin{aligned} s_n - s_n' &= (a_1 - b_1)10^{-1} + (a_2 - b_2)10^{-2} \\ &\quad + \cdots + (a_q - b_q)10^{-q} + \cdots + (a_s - b_s)10^{-s} \\ &\quad + \cdots + (a_n - b_n)10^{-n} \\ &\geq (a_q - b_q)10^{-q} - 9(10^{-q-1} + \cdots + 10^{-n}) + 10^{-s} \\ &\geq 10^{-q} - 10^{-q} + 10^{-s} = 10^{-s}. \end{aligned}$$

Since, for all n, $s_n - s_n' > 10^{-s}$, the limit $\alpha - \beta$ of $s_n - s_n'$ must be $\geq 10^{-s} > 0$. Hence, the limit is not 0, and the lemma is proved.

LEMMA 4. *If* $a_i = b_i$ *for* $1 \leq i < k$; $a_k = b_k + 1$; *and* $a_i = 0$, $b_i = 9$ *for* $i > k$, *then*

$$.a_1 a_2 \cdots = .b_1 b_2 \cdots .$$

Proof: Let s_n, s_n' be as in the preceding proof. Then for $n > k$,

$$
\begin{aligned}
s_n - s_n' &= (a_k - b^k)10^{-k} + \cdots + (a_n - b_n)10^{-n} \\
&= 10^{-k} - 9(10^{-k-1} + \cdots + 10^{-n}) \\
&= 10^{-k} - 9(10/9)(10^{-k-1} - 10^{-n-1}) = 10^{-n}.
\end{aligned}
$$

Since $10^{-n} \to 0$, also $s_n - s_n' \to 0$, which proves the lemma.

Lemmas 3 and 4 along with exercise 4, p. 111, complete the discussion of the conditions under which two decimals may be equal.

We now ask, which decimals correspond to rational numbers? We begin the investigation by asking first if the decimals, obtained from rational numbers, by way of the proof of Lemma 2, p. 107, have any characteristic features. While reading the following discussion the reader might find it useful to examine the division carried out on p. 000.

Let $\alpha = p/q$ be a rational number between 0 and 1, and suppose $\alpha = .a_1 a_2 \cdots$, where the a_i have been chosen as in the proof of Lemma 2. That is,

$$a_1 \leq 10\alpha < a_1 + 1;$$
$$a_n \leq 10^n(\alpha - a_1 10^{-1} - a_2 10^{-2} - \cdots - a_{n-1} 10^{-n+1}) < a_n + 1.$$

We set

$$10^n(\alpha - a_1 10^{-1} - a_2 10^{-2} - \cdots - a_{n-1} 10^{-n+1}) = Q_n/q$$

and note that Q_n is an integer. An elementary calculation proves

$$Q_{n+1}/q = 10(Q_n/q - a_n). \tag{*}$$

Since

$$a_n \leq Q_n/q < a_n + 1, \tag{**}$$

we have $a_n q \leq Q_n < a_n q + q$, and therefore,

$$Q_n = a_n q + r_n, \qquad 0 \leq r_n < q.$$

Since there are only ten possible values for a_n (namely, $0, 1, 2, \cdots, 9$) and q possible values for r_n (namely, $0, 1, 2, \cdots, q - 1$), there are only $10q$ possible values for Q_n. But there are indefinitely many Q_n, so there must be two, say Q_s and Q_{s+t}, that are equal. From $Q_s = Q_{s+t}$ and (∗∗) we conclude (see exercise 3, p. 105) that $a_s = a_{s+t}$. From this and (∗) we find

$$Q_{s+1}/q = 10(Q_s/q - a_s) = 10(Q_{s+t}/q - a_{s+t}) = Q_{s+t+1}/q,$$

which (as above) yields $a_{s+1} = a_{s+t+1}$. An induction argument yields

$$a_{s+j} = a_{s+t+j} \text{ for all } j \geq 0.$$

This means

$$\alpha = .a_1 a_2 \cdots a_{s-1} a_s \cdots a_{s+t} a_s \cdots a_{s+t} a_s \cdots a_{s+t} \cdots .$$

That is, the decimal for α is *periodic* with repeating part $a_s \cdots a_{s+t}$. This proves the following lemma.

LEMMA 5. *Every rational number has a periodic decimal expansion.*

● E X A M P L E. To illustrate the proof we carry out on the right, the usual mechanical algorithm leading to the decimal expansion of the fraction $117/140$. We have circled the "remainders" r_i. In this example

$$Q_1 = 1170,$$
$$r_1 = 50,$$
$$Q_2 = 500,$$
$$r_2 = 80,$$
$$Q_3 = 800,$$
$$r_3 = 100,$$

and so on. Also, $s = 3$, $t = 6$. We write

$$117/140 = .83\dot{5}7142\dot{8},$$

where the dots over the 5 and 8 indicate that this block is repeated indefinitely often.

The converse proposition is also true.

```
            .83571428···
140/117.00000000···
    1120
    (500)
     420
    (800) ←
     700
    (1000)
     980
     200
     140
    (600)
     560
    (400)
     280
    (1200)
     1120
    (800) ←
          ···
```

same remainder

LEMMA 6.   *The decimal* $.a_1 \cdots a_s \dot{b}_1 \cdots \dot{b}_t$ *is the expansion of a rational number.*

Proof: See exercise 6, below.

● EXERCISES

1. Prove that the a_n appearing in the proof of Lemma 2 are all greater than or equal to 0 and less than or equal to 9. [*Hint:* Use an induction argument.]

2. (a) In Lemma 1 replace 10 by k (where k is a positive integer greater than 1) and 9 by $k - 1$ and prove the resulting statement.

(b) Reinterpret Lemma 2 in accordance with the modified Lemma 1 and prove.

3. Look up Cantor's theorem in reference 12 (see p. 142), and discuss the results of Section VI.5 in the light of that theorem.

4. (a) Prove that two distinct nonterminating decimals are unequal.

(b) Prove that two distinct terminating decimals are unequal.

5. Where in the proof of Lemma 3 did we use the hypothesis that the decimal $.a_1 a_2 \cdots$ does not end in all nines? [*Hint:* Examine closely the two sentences beginning with the phrase "without loss of generality."]

6. Prove Lemma 6, above. [*Hint:* Exercise 9, p. 103, might prove helpful.]

7. Find integers p and q such that p/q is equal to:

(i) $.12\dot{3}4\dot{5}$;

(ii) $.\dot{1}4685239\dot{7}$;

(iii) $.742\dot{8}\dot{9}$.

8. (a) Prove that the number $.01001000100001 \cdots$ is not rational.

(b) Using this as a paradigm can you construct other non-rational decimals?

(c) Give a formula which can be used to calculate the nth digit of the decimal in (a).

9. Justify all the steps in the following proof of Lemmas 3 and 4. (We denote the limit of a convergent sequence, say $\{c_n\}$, by

lim c_n.) Suppose $\alpha = .a_1a_2\cdots$, $\beta = .b_1b_2\cdots$ and suppose that these decimals do not have the same digits but $\alpha = \beta$. Let q be the smallest subscript such that $a_q \neq b_q$ and suppose without loss of generality that $a_q < b_q$. Then, for $n > q$, $\lim (a_q10^{-q} + \cdots + a_n10^{-n})$ $= a_q10^{-q} + \lim(a_{q+1}10^{-q-1} + \cdots + a_n10^{-n}) \leq a_q10^{-q}$ $+ 9\lim(10^{-q-1} + \cdots + 10^{-n}) = a_q10^{-q} + 10^{-q} = (a_q + 1)10^{-q}$ $\leq b_q10^{-q} \leq \lim(b_q10^{-q} + \cdots + b_n10^{-n})$.

Hence, since $\alpha = \beta$, all inequalities are equalities. From this it follows that $a_i = 9$ and $b_i = 0$ for $i > q$.

Cardinal Numbers (continued)

In the appendix to Chapter III we introduced finite and infinite sets, finite cardinal numbers, and the cardinal number $\aleph_0$. In this appendix we continue our discussion of cardinal numbers and, among other things, we shall prove the existence of infinite sets which do not have cardinal number $\aleph_0$, that is of nonempty sets which are not equivalent to Z nor to any S_n. Indeed, we shall show that the set $R^{\#}$ of real numbers is infinite but does not have cardinal number $\aleph_0$.

A.1. Cardinal Inequalities

We begin our discussion with a definition in which we introduce the notions of a pair of sets having the same "cardinality" and of a set having "greater cardinality" than another set.

DEFINITION. *Let* A *and* B *be two sets. Then:*

(i) *we write* $A \overset{c}{\leq} B$ *if* $A \sim B'$ *for* B′ *some subset of* B;

(ii) *we write* $A \overset{c}{=} B$ *if* $A \sim B$;

(iii) *we write* $A \overset{c}{<} B$ *if* $A \overset{c}{\leq} B$ *and not* $A \sim B$.

When $A \overset{c}{=} B$ *we say that* A *and* B *have the same cardinality, and when* $A \overset{c}{<} B$ *we say that* B *has greater cardinality than* A. *Notice that if* n, m *are in* Z *and* $n < m$, *then*

$$S_n \overset{c}{<} S_m \overset{c}{<} Z.$$

These inequalities are easily proved using material from Sections 2 and 3 of the appendix to Chapter III.

We wish next to prove that there is no set of greatest cardinality. That is, given any set A there exists a set B such that $A \overset{c}{<} B$. The proof will involve a technique which is very useful in set theory, but which is somewhat difficult for the beginner to follow. Because of this, immediately following the proof we give a simple example which illustrates the details of the proof. By referring back and forth from proof to example the reader should be able to grasp the essential idea without difficulty.

THEOREM. *Given any set* A *there exists a set* B *such that* $A \overset{c}{<} B$.

Proof: The following proof is for sets A containing at least two elements. For other sets the theorem is obvious. Let A be a given set and let B be the set of all mappings of A into A. We shall show first that $A \sim B'$, where B' is a certain subset of B. Then we shall show that $A \sim B$ is false.

Let B' be the set of all "constant" mappings of A into A, that is, all mappings for which there is but a single image element. If the single image element of a mapping in B' is a, we denote the mapping by I_a. Since for each a in A there is such an I_a, we clearly have $A \sim B'$. This proves the first part.

To prove $A \sim B$ is false, we shall show that every mapping of A into B fails to be 1 to 1. To this end, let g be an arbitrary mapping of A into B. (Thus, for each a in A, $g(a)$ is a mapping of A into A.) We show that g is not 1 to 1. Let a_1, a_2 be distinct elements of A (A has at least two elements by hypothesis). Define the mapping F of A into A by

$$F(a) = a_1 \text{ if } g(a) \text{ does not map } a \text{ into } a_1;$$
$$F(a) = a_2 \text{ if } g(a) \text{ does map } a \text{ into } a_1.$$

Clearly, F is a mapping of A into A which differs from every mapping $g(a)$, of A into A. In fact, F differs at a from the mapping $g(a)$. Therefore, g is not 1 to 1, and $A \sim B$ is false. This completes the proof of the theorem.

● E X A M P L E.   Let $A = \{1, 2\}$. Then $B = \{f_1, f_2, f_3, f_4\}$, where f_1, f_2, f_3, f_4 are defined by the pictures below. Clearly, B is the set of all mappings of A into A. Let g be a mapping of A into B.

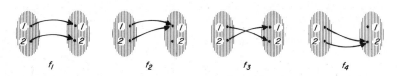

Define F by:

$$F(1) = \begin{cases} 1 \text{ if } g(1) \text{ does not map 1 into 1;} \\ 2 \text{ if } g(1) \text{ does map 1 into 1.} \end{cases}$$

$$F(2) = \begin{cases} 1 \text{ if } g(2) \text{ does not map 2 into 1;} \\ 2 \text{ if } g(2) \text{ does map 2 into 1.} \end{cases}$$

For instance, if $g(1) = f_1$ and $g(2) = f_2$, then

$$F(1) = 2,$$
$$F(2) = 2,$$

and therefore $F = f_4$, which is distinct from f_1 and f_2.

COROLLARY 1. *If a set has at least two elements, the set of all mappings of the set into itself has greater cardinality than the set.*

COROLLARY 2. *There exist infinite sets that do not have cardinality* $\aleph_0$.

Proof: Consider the nonempty set A of all mappings of Z into Z. The subset of constant mappings is equivalent to Z, so by exercise 6(b), p. 61, the set A is infinite. By the first corollary, $Z \overset{c}{<} A$. Therefore, $A \sim Z$ is false, and A does not have cardinality $\aleph_0$.

LEMMA. *Every infinite set contains a subset equivalent to Z.*

Proof: Let A be an infinite set. Then there is at least one element, say a_1, in A. Consider the set A_1 consisting of A with a_1 removed. Since A is infinite, it is not the case that $A \sim S_1$. Hence, A_1 is nonempty. Let a_2 be an element of A_1. Consider the set A_2 consisting of A_1 with a_2 removed. Since A is infinite, it is not the case that $A \sim S_2$. Hence, A_2 is nonempty. We continue and find a sequence $a_1, a_2, \cdots$ of elements all in A. The subset $B = \{a_1, a_2, \cdots\}$ of A is clearly equivalent to Z, and the lemma is proved. (For a discussion of the basic principle underlying this proof we refer the reader to a discussion of the "axiom of choice." See, for example, reference 16.)

COROLLARY.   *If* A *is an infinite set, then* $Z \stackrel{c}{\leq} A$.

A.2. The Cardinal Number $\mathfrak{c}$

In the last section we showed that given any set there is another with greater cardinality. In this section we prove that the set of real numbers $R^\#$ has greater cardinality than the set Z. The proof we use was first given by Georg Cantor.

Actually, what Cantor proved (and what we imitate) was that the set of real numbers G which are greater than zero and less than 1 is of greater cardinality than Z, that is, $Z \stackrel{c}{<} G$. Since G is contained in $R^\#$, we know, by exercise 4, p. 123, that $Z \stackrel{c}{<} R^\#$ once we have proved $Z \stackrel{c}{<} G$.

THEOREM. $Z \stackrel{c}{<} G$.

Proof: We must prove two things: that $Z \sim G'$ for some subset G' of G and that $Z \sim G$ is false. The first is easy, since we may take $G' = \{1/2, 1/3, 1/4, \cdots\}$ and map Z onto G' by the mapping taking n into $1/(n + 1)$. This is clearly a 1 to 1 mapping, so $Z \sim G'$. To prove $Z \sim G$ is false, we show that every mapping of Z into G fails to be 1 to 1.

We make use of the decimal expansions of the elements of G. (In the cases where an element of G has two decimal expansions we choose the one ending in nines.) Let f be a mapping of Z into G. Then we have

$$f(1) = 0.a_{11}a_{12}a_{13}a_{14}\cdots,$$
$$f(2) = 0.a_{21}a_{22}a_{23}a_{24}\cdots,$$
$$f(3) = 0.a_{31}a_{32}a_{33}a_{34}\cdots,$$
$$\cdots\cdots\cdots\cdots\cdots\cdots\cdots\cdots\cdots,$$
$$f(n) = 0.a_{n1}a_{n2}a_{n3}a_{n4}\cdots,$$
$$\cdots\cdots\cdots\cdots\cdots\cdots\cdots\cdots\cdots,$$

where each a_{ij} is an integer between 0 and 9 inclusive. We show that f is not a 1 to 1 mapping of Z onto G by exhibiting a real number in G which is not the image of any element of Z. Indeed, the real number $b = 0.b_1b_2b_3\cdots$, where

$$b_n = \begin{cases} 5 \text{ if } a_{nn} \neq 5, \\ 6 \text{ if } a_{nn} = 5, \end{cases}$$

is not the image of any m, since, if

$$f(m) = b,$$

then

$$0.a_{m1}a_{m2}a_{m3} \cdots = 0.b_1b_2b_3 \cdots,$$

and therefore the digits would have to be the same (see exercise 4(a), p. 111). In particular we would necessarily have

$$a_{mm} = b_m.$$

But this is false by the definition of the b_i. Therefore, f is not 1 to 1, and the theorem is proved.

DEFINITION. *A set is said to have cardinal number $\mathfrak{c}$ if it is equivalent to* G.

Remark. In Section A.1 we found that if A was any infinite set, then $Z \overset{c}{\leq} A$. We have now found that $Z \overset{c}{<} G$. A natural question is: Does there exist an infinite set A such that $Z \overset{c}{<} A \overset{c}{<} G$? The answer to this question is not known. It is generally assumed that no such set exists. This assumption is called the "continuum hypothesis."

When $n < m$ we may now write

$$S_n \overset{c}{<} S_m \overset{c}{<} Z \overset{c}{<} G.$$

Ordinarily, however, it would be preferrable to write

$$n < m < \aleph_0 < \mathfrak{c}. \tag{$*$}$$

Because of this we make the following convention, which justifies ($*$).

If the sets A and B have the cardinal numbers α and β, respectively, and if $A \overset{c}{<} B$, we shall write $\alpha < \beta$.

In a more advanced discussion one defines a cardinal number for every set and proves that the relation $<$ introduced between cardinal numbers is a linear ordering relation. Because of technical difficulties not easily overcome in a brief introduction we omit this part of the theory. Thus, in our discussion the only sets with defined cardinal numbers are the finite sets and those sets equivalent to either Z or G.

A.3. Other Sets of Cardinality $\mathfrak{c}$

We begin with a simple lemma.

LEMMA.   *We can add or remove a single element from an infinite set without changing its cardinality.*

Proof: Let A be an infinite set. We select a sequence $a_1, a_2, \cdots$ from A.

(a) Let s be an element not in A and let A_1 be the set A with s adjoined. Define the mapping f of A onto A_1 by:

$$\begin{cases} f(a_1) = s; \\ f(a_i) = a_{i-1} \text{ for } i \geq 2; \\ f(t) \ \ = t \text{ for all other } t \text{ in A.} \end{cases}$$

Clearly, f is 1 to 1, so $A \sim A_1$.

(b) Suppose that A_2 is the set remaining when the element q is removed from A. The sequence $a_1, a_2, \cdots$ selected from A could have been chosen such that $a_1 = q$. We assume it was. Define the mapping g of A onto A_2 by:

$$\begin{cases} g(q) \ \ = a_2; \\ g(a_i) = a_{i+1} \text{ for } i \geq 2; \\ g(t) \ \ = t \text{ for all other } t \text{ in A.} \end{cases}$$

Clearly, g is 1 to 1, so $A \sim A_2$.

Parts (a) and (b) complete the proof of the lemma.

COROLLARY.   *Adding or removing a finite number of elements from an infinite set does not change its cardinality.*

LEMMA.   *Adding a set of cardinality $\aleph_0$ to an infinite set does not change its cardinality.*

We leave the proof of this lemma to exercise 10, p. 124.

We introduce the following notations when $a < b;\, a, b$ in $R^{\#}$:

(a, b) is the set of all real numbers $x, a < x < b$;
$[a, b)$ is the set of all real numbers $x, a \leq x < b$;
$(a, b]$ is the set of all real numbers $x, a < x \leq b$;
$[a, b]$ is the set of all real numbers $x, a \leq x \leq b$.

We call these sets of numbers *intervals*. When we use the word interval it will mean a set of real numbers of one of these four types.

LEMMA.   *If $a < b$, then $(0, 1) \sim (a, b)$.*

Proof: We define the mapping f of (a, b) onto $(0, 1)$ by

$$f(x) = \frac{x - a}{b - a}, \ x \text{ in } (a, b).$$

This mapping is best described by the accompanying graph.

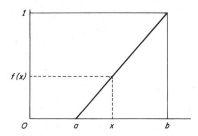

COROLLARY.   *Every interval has cardinality* $\mathfrak{c}$.

Proof: By the first lemma of this section, p. 118.

$$(a, b) \sim [a, b) \sim (a, b] \sim [a, b],$$

By the lemma, $(a, b) \sim (0, 1)$. Hence all these intervals have cardinality $\mathfrak{c}$, and the corollary is proved.

LEMMA. $R^{\#}$ *has cardinality* $\mathfrak{c}$.

Proof: Define the mapping f of G into $R^{\#}$ by:

$$f(x) = \begin{cases} 1/2x - 1 \text{ for } 0 < x < 1/2; \\ 1/(2x - 2) + 1 \text{ for } 1/2 \le x < 1. \end{cases}$$

This mapping is clearly 1 to 1, as can be seen by examining the graph on p. 120.

A.4. Cardinal Arithmetic

We turn our attention to the *arithmetic* of cardinal numbers. We are all familiar with the fact that finite cardinal numbers can

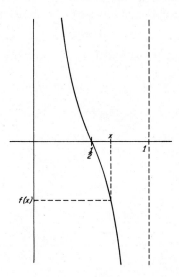

be added and multiplied. We wish to extend these operations so
they will apply also to infinite cardinal numbers (such as $\aleph_0$ and $\mathfrak{c}$).
Though our discussion will be restricted to the finite cardinal num-
bers and $\aleph_0$ and $\mathfrak{c}$, our definitions are general. Let us consider
addition first.

One way of determining the sum of two finite cardinal numbers,
say m and n, is to proceed as follows. Take a set A with m elements
and another set B with n elements and consider the set C whose
elements are those of A along with those of B. Then the number of
elements in C is the sum of m and n. We make precise this method
of addition of cardinal numbers and at the same time phrase it
so that it applies to the sum of any two cardinal numbers, finite
or not.

DEFINITION. *Let α and β be cardinal numbers. Choose disjoint sets A and B with cardinal numbers α and β, respectively (see
exercise 12, p. 124). Then $\alpha + \beta$ is defined to be the cardinal number*

of the set C *containing precisely the elements of* A *along with those of* B. (The set C is called the "set union" of A and B. See exercise 5, p. 24.)

Note carefully that the definition of $\alpha + \beta$ does *not* depend upon the sets A and B. Any other disjoint sets with the same cardinal numbers would yield the same result.

We leave the verification of the following three properties of addition to the reader.

(a) If α and β are finite cardinal numbers, then $\alpha + \beta$ is the expected finite cardinal number;

(b) $\alpha + \beta = \beta + \alpha$;

(c) $(\alpha + \beta) + \gamma = \alpha + (\beta + \gamma)$.

The following lemma puts forth the simplest results obtainable by adding the cardinal numbers we have defined.

LEMMA.   (i) $n + \alpha = \alpha$, *for* n *a finite and* α *an infinite cardinal number;*

(ii) $\aleph_0 + \aleph_0 = \aleph_0$;

(iii) $\aleph_0 + \mathfrak{c} = \mathfrak{c}$;

(iv) $\mathfrak{c} + \mathfrak{c} = \mathfrak{c}$.

Proof: (i) By the corollary, p. 118.

(ii) Let $A = \{1, 3, 5, 7, \cdots\}$, $B = \{2, 4, 6, 8, \cdots\}$. Then $\alpha = \beta = \aleph_0$, and $C = Z$. Hence, $\aleph_0 + \aleph_0 = \aleph_0$.

(iii) By the second lemma in Section A.3, p. 118.

(iv) Since $(0, 1)$ is the set union of $(0, 1/2]$ and $(1/2, 1)$ and each of these intervals has cardinality $\mathfrak{c}$, the conclusion follows.

We now define multiplication for cardinal numbers. The definition must, of course, give rise to results that agree with the ordinary products of finite cardinal numbers.

DEFINITION.   *Let* α *and* β *be cardinal numbers. Let* A *and* B *be sets with cardinal numbers* α *and* β, *respectively. Then the cardinal number* $\alpha\beta$ *is the cardinal number of the cartesian product set* $A \times B$.

Once again, note carefully that the definition of $\alpha\beta$ does *not* depend upon the sets A and B. Any other sets with the same cardinal numbers would yield the same result.

We leave the verification of the following properties to the reader.

(a) If α and β are finite cardinal numbers, then $\alpha\beta$ is the expected finite cardinal number;

(b) $\alpha\beta = \beta\alpha$;

(c) $(\alpha\beta)\gamma = \alpha(\beta\gamma)$;

(d) $\alpha(\beta + \gamma) = \alpha\beta + \alpha\gamma$.

The following lemma puts forth the simplest results obtainable by multiplying the cardinal numbers we have defined.

LEMMA.   (i) $m \; \aleph_0 = \aleph_0$ for m in Z;

              (ii) $\aleph_0 \aleph_0 = \aleph_0$;

              (iii) $\aleph_0 \mathfrak{c} = \mathfrak{c}$;

              (iv) $\mathfrak{c}\mathfrak{c} = \mathfrak{c}$.

Proof: (i) Let $A = \{1, 2, 3, \cdots, m\}$, $B = Z$. Then

$$A \times B = \{(1, 1), (1, 2), (1, 3), \cdots$$
$$(2, 1), (2, 2), (2, 3), \cdots$$
$$\cdots\cdots\cdots\cdots\cdots\cdots\cdots\cdots$$
$$(m, 1), (m, 2), (m, 3), \cdots\}.$$

We map $A \times B$ onto Z by f, where

$$f((i, j)) = (j - 1)m + i.$$

A little reflection quickly reveals this to be a 1 to 1 mapping. Hence, $A \times B$ has cardinality $\aleph_0$, and (i) is proved. (The mapping f merely counts the elements of $A \times B$ by columns.)

(ii) Let $A = B = Z$. Then $A \times B = Z \times Z$, and we have shown in the appendix to Chapter III (see pp. 60–61) that $Z \times Z$ has cardinal number $\aleph_0$. This proves (ii).

(iii) Let $A = \{\cdots, -3, -2, -1, 0, 1, 2, 3, \cdots\}$ and $B = [0, 1)$. Then we define the mapping f of $A \times B$ onto $R^{\#}$ by

$$f((k, b)) = k + b.$$

Clearly, this is a 1 to 1 mapping, so $A \times B$ has cardinality $\mathfrak{c}$, which proves (iii).

(iv) The proof of this is carried out in exercise 15, p. 124.

Even though we have barely scratched the surface of the theory of "transfinite" cardinal numbers we must now draw this appendix to a close. There are a number of excellent books the reader may consult if he wishes to continue his study along these lines. Some of them are listed on p. 142. We particularly recommend reference 16 by Sierpinski.

● EXERCISES

1. Prove $A \overset{c}{<} B$, $A \overset{c}{=} C$, $B \overset{c}{=} D$ implies $C \overset{c}{<} D$.

2. Prove: $A \overset{c}{<} A$ is false for every set A.

3. Prove: $A \overset{c}{<} B$, $B \overset{c}{<} C$ implies $A \overset{c}{<} C$.

4. Prove: $A \overset{c}{<} B$ and B is a subset of C, then $A \overset{c}{<} C$. [*Hint:* If $C \sim A$, then B would be equivalent to some subset of A contrary to $A \overset{c}{<} B$.]

5. Prove: $S_n \overset{c}{<} S_m \overset{c}{<} Z$ when $n < m$.

6. For the example after the proof of the theorem in Section A.1 fill in the table of F's, on the right, for various choices of $g(1)$, $g(2)$. We have filled in the spot computed in the text.

$g(1)$ $\diagdown$ $g(2)$	f_1	f_2	f_3	f_4
f_1		f_4		
f_2				
f_3				
f_4				

7. (a) Prove that the number of subsets of S_n is 2^n;

(b) Prove that the number of mappings of S_n into S_n is n^n.

8. Let S be a set with at least two elements and let $\bar{S}$ be the set of mappings of S into S. Further, let 2^S be the set of subsets of S. Prove $2^S \overset{c}{\leq} \bar{S}$.

[*Hint:* Let s_1, s_2 be distinct elements of S. For each A in 2^S define F_A in $\bar{S}$ as follows:

$$F_A(a) = \begin{cases} s_1 \text{ for } a \text{ in A}; \\ s_2 \text{ for } a \text{ not in A}. \end{cases}$$

Then $F_A \neq F_B$ for $A \neq B$, and clearly $2^S \sim C$ for some subset C of $\bar{S}$.]

9. Let S and 2^S be as in exercise 8. Show $S \overset{c}{<} 2^S$.

[*Hint:* To prove $S \sim 2^S$ is false, show that every mapping g of S into 2^S fails to be 1 to 1. To do this, define a subset A of S as follows: a is in A if and only if $g(a)$ does not contain a. Then clearly A is a subset of S, but $A \neq g(a)$ for any a.]

10. Prove the corollary to the first lemma in Section A.3 and also prove the second lemma in this section.

11. *Exhibit* a 1 to 1 mapping of $(0, 1)$ onto $(0, 1]$.

12. Let A, B have cardinal numbers α, β, respectively. Show the existence of disjoint sets A', B' which have cardinal numbers α, β, respectively.

13. Show that the definitions of $\alpha + \beta$ and $\alpha\beta$ do *not* depend on the particular sets A and B chosen in the definitions of these operations.

14. Prove properties (b) and (c), p. 121, of cardinal addition and properties (b), (c), and (d), p. 122, of cardinal multiplication.

15. (a) Prove that every real number $x, 0 < x \leq 1$, has a unique (dyadic) representation in the form

$$x = 2^{-n_1} + 2^{-n_1-n_2} + 2^{-n_1-n_2-n_3} + \cdots ,$$

where the n_i are positive integers.

(b) Let S denote the set of all sequences of positive integers. Prove that the cardinality of S is $\mathfrak{c}$.

(c) Prove that S defined in (b) satisfies

$$S \times S \sim S;$$

(d) Conclude from (c) that $\mathfrak{c}\mathfrak{c} = \mathfrak{c}$.

[*Hint:* Part (a) can be proved in the same way we proved the corresponding theorem with 2 replaced by 10 (see exercise 2(b), p. 111). The representation given in (a) can be used to define a 1 to 1 map from $(0, 1]$ onto S to prove (b). To prove (c), map the element (s, t) of $S \times S$, where $s = \{n_1, n_2, \cdots\}$, $t = \{m_1, m_2, \cdots\}$, onto the element $\{n_1, m_1, n_2, m_2, \cdots\}$ of S and prove this is a 1 to 1 mapping.]

16. Let $A \subset B$ mean the set A is a subset of the set B. Consider the two propositions:

(I) $A \sim D$ and $A \subset C \subset D$ implies $A \sim C$.

(II) If each of A and B is similar to a subset of the other, then $A \sim B$.

Deduce (II) from (I). [Actually, (I) and (II) are equivalent. Proposition (II) is called the Cantor–Bernstein theorem. For a proof, consult the books by Kamke and Sierpinski listed on p. 142.]

17. Prove $n\mathfrak{c} = \mathfrak{c}$ for n in $\mathbf{Z}$.

APPENDIX B
The Complex Numbers

In the course of our construction of the real numbers we have passed through several stages as indicated below.

$$(Z; +, \cdot) \rightarrow (R; +, \cdot) \rightarrow (R^+; +, \cdot) \rightarrow (R^\#; +, \cdot).$$

Here, each system is an extension of the preceding one. In each case a partial motivation for wishing an extension was the non-solvability of certain kinds of algebraic equations. Thus, the algebraic equation:

$$5x = 3 \begin{cases} \text{cannot be solved in } (Z; +, \cdot), \\ \text{but can be solved in } (R; +, \cdot); \end{cases}$$

$$x^2 = 2 \begin{cases} \text{cannot be solved in } (R; +, \cdot), \\ \text{but can be solved in } (R^+; +, \cdot); \end{cases}$$

$$5 + x = 3 \begin{cases} \text{cannot be solved in } (R^+; +, \cdot), \\ \text{but can be solved in } (R^\#; +, \cdot). \end{cases}$$

Because of the position in which we have placed the solvability of algebraic equations it is legitimate to ask if we have arrived, with the system $(R^\#; +, \cdot)$, at a place where all algebraic equations are solvable. We have not. This is readily seen by considering the equation $x^2 = -1$. Since $0^2 = 0$, and every nonzero number when squared is positive, the square of no number in $R^\#$ is -1. Therefore, $x^2 = -1$ is not solvable in $R^\#$. In this appendix we extend the system $(R^\#; +, \cdot)$ so that the equation $x^2 = -1$ has a solution in the larger system. This larger system is called *the complex number system*.

Again we might ask: "Are we now finished, or are there equations like $x^3 = -13$ or $5x^2 + 17x - 31 = 0$ or $x^{100} - x^{48} + 5 = 0$, and so on, not solvable in the complex numbers?" An important theorem of algebra (sometimes called the fundamental theorem of algebra—first proved by Gauss in 1799) assures us that in a certain sense the complex numbers are the end of the line. We shall state this theorem after we make the extension. We proceed to the details.

Define C to be the set of all ordered pairs of real numbers. That is,

$$C = R^{\#} \times R^{\#}.$$

The elements of C will be called *complex numbers*. We note that the complex numbers (a, b) and (c, d) are *equal* if and only if

$$a = c \text{ and } b = d.$$

We introduce two operations, denoted by $\oplus$ and $\odot$, respectively, into C by:

$$(a, b) \oplus (c, d) = (a + c, b + d);$$
$$(a, b) \odot (c, d) = (ac - bd, ad + bc).$$

It is clear that the algebraic system $(C; \oplus, \odot)$ is closed with respect to both of the operations. The following lemma is true, and we leave its (mechanical) verification to the reader.

LEMMA 1.　(a) $\oplus$ *is commutative and associative;*
　　　　　　(b) $\odot$ *is commutative and associative;*
　　　　　　(c) $\odot$ *is distributive over* $\oplus$.

By direct computation we see that $(0, 0)$ is a $\oplus$-identity and $(1, 0)$ is a $\odot$-identity. Indeed,

$$(a, b) \oplus (0, 0) = (a, b);$$
$$(a, b) \odot (1, 0) = (a, b).$$

The next two lemmas prove the existence of "inverse operations" for each of the operations $\oplus$ and $\odot$.

LEMMA 2.　*Let* α *and* β *be in* C. *Then the equation* $\beta \oplus x = \alpha$ *has a unique solution for* x *in* C.

Proof: Let $\alpha = (a, b)$ and $\beta = (c, d)$. Then for $x = (y, z)$ to satisfy the equation we must have

$$\beta \oplus x = (c, d) \oplus (y, z) = (c + y, d + z) = (a, b).$$

Hence,
$$c + y = a,$$
$$d + z = b.$$

This means that if (y, z) satisfies the equation, then

$$y = a - c \text{ and } z = b - d.$$

Thus there is at most one solution. Since $x = (a - c, b - d)$ does satisfy the equation, the lemma is proved.

The unique solution of $\beta \oplus x = \alpha$, whose existence is guaranteed by Lemma 2, is denoted by $\alpha \ominus \beta$. By the proof of that lemma we have

$$(a, b) \ominus (c, d) = (a - c, b - d).$$

LEMMA 3. *Let α and β, $\beta \neq (0, 0)$, be in C. Then the equation $\beta \odot x = \alpha$ has a unique solution for x in C.*

Proof: Let $\alpha = (a, b)$ and $\beta = (c, d)$. Then for $x = (y, z)$ to satisfy the equation we must have

$$\beta \odot x = (c, d) \odot (y, z) = (cy - dz, cz + dy) = (a, b).$$

Hence,
$$cy - dz = a;$$
$$dy + cz = b.$$

Solving these simultaneous equations gives

$$y = (ac + bd)/(c^2 + d^2),$$
$$z = (bc - ad)/(c^2 + d^2).$$

This means that for $x = (y, z)$ to satisfy the equation y and z must be given by these expressions. Since $x = (y, z)$ does satisfy the equation, when y and z are as given, the proof is complete.

The unique solution of $\beta \odot x = \alpha$, $\beta \neq (0, 0)$, whose existence is guaranteed by Lemma 3, is denoted by $\alpha \oslash \beta$. By the proof of that lemma

$$(a, b) \oslash (c, d) = ((ac + bd)/(c^2 + d^2), (bc - ad)/(c^2 + d^2)).$$

We now single out the subset $\mathrm{R}_{\mathrm{C}}^{\#}$ of all elements (a, b) in C for which $b = 0$. Then, clearly $(\mathrm{R}_{\mathrm{C}}^{\#}; \oplus, \odot)$ is an algebraic system, and further, since

$$(a, 0) \oplus (b, 0) = (a + b, 0),$$

and
$$(a, 0) \odot (b, 0) = (ab, 0),$$

this system is closed with respect to both operations. Indeed, more is true, as we see in the following lemma.

LEMMA 4. $(R_C^{\#}; \oplus, \odot) \cong (R^{\#}; +, \cdot)$.

Proof: Define the mapping f of $R^{\#}$ into $R_C^{\#}$ by
$$f(a) = (a, 0).$$

Clearly, f is a 1 to 1 mapping. Since
$$f(a + b) = (a + b, 0) = (a, 0) \oplus (b, 0) = f(a) \oplus f(b)$$
and
$$f(ab) = (ab, 0) = (a, 0) \odot (b, 0) = f(a) \cdot f(b)$$

f is also an isomorphism, and the lemma is proved.

In view of Lemma 4 we may discard the system $(R^{\#}; +, \cdot)$ in favor of the system $(R_C^{\#}; \oplus, \odot)$. Thus, we will no longer need the names of the real numbers and shall use these names for the corresponding elements of $R_C^{\#}$. Thus, we shall use, for example, 2, -1, and $1/4$ for $(2, 0)$, $(-1, 0)$, and $(1/4, 0)$, respectively. We will even write $2 = (2, 0)$, and so on. In general,
$$a = (a, 0).$$

We make one further convention regarding the names of elements of C. We shall designate the element $(0, 1)$ by i. Making use of these conventions we have
$$(0, b) = (b, 0) \odot (0, 1) = b \odot i.$$

Therefore, we also have
$$(a, b) = (a, 0) \oplus (0, b) = a \oplus (b \odot i).$$

We make one final notational simplification. Since we have abandoned the system of real numbers, we no longer need $+$ and $\cdot$ for the addition and multiplication of real numbers. Therefore, we adopt these symbols to replace the more cumbersome $\oplus$ and $\odot$ in C. Thus, from now on we deal with the system $(C; +, \cdot)$. In this system the last equation above becomes
$$(a, b) = (a, 0) + (0, b) = a + bi.$$

From now on we *always* write our complex numbers in the $a + bi$ form. We collect below the basic operational formulas used in working with complex numbers. They are all given above, but we put them here into the conventional notations. (Note that we use $-$ and $/$ for $\ominus$ and $\oslash$ of the above.)

$$(a + bi) + (c + di) = (a + c) + (b + d)i;$$
$$(a + bi) \cdot (c + di) = (ac - bd) + (bc + ad)i;$$
$$(a + bi) - (c + di) = (a - c) + (b - d)i;$$

$$(a + bi)/(c + di) = \frac{ac + bd}{c^2 + d^2} + \frac{bc - ad}{c^2 + d^2} i, \text{ when } c^2 + d^2 \neq 0.$$

We have then constructed an algebraic system $(C; +, \cdot)$, which is an extension of the system $(R^{\#}; +, \cdot)$. In this system we see that

$$i^2 = i \cdot i = (0 + 1i) \cdot (0 + 1i) = (0 - 1) + (0 + 0)i = -1.$$

Hence, the equation $x^2 = -1$ has a solution in C, namely $x = i$. Also, $x = -i$ is a solution of this equation. There are no other solutions.

We now state the fundamental theorem of algebra.

THEOREM.   *Let n be a positive integer and let $a_0, a_1, \cdots, a_n$ be arbitrary complex numbers. Then there exists a complex number x such that*

$$a_n x^n + a_{n-1} x^{n-1} + \cdots + a_1 x + a_0 = 0.$$

There is no really simple proof of this theorem. In each of references 1 and 2 (p. 142) will be found a discussion of this theorem. However, for the most elementary proof of the theorem the reader should consult the paper by Raymond Redheffer, "The Fundamental Theorem of Algebra," *The American Mathematical Monthly*, vol. 64, 8 (1957), pp. 582–585.

● EXERCISES

1. Prove Lemma 1.

2. Where in the proof of Lemma 3 did we use the hypothesis that $\beta \neq (0, 0)$?

3. Prove that there are only two complex number solutions of the equation $x^2 = -1$.

4. Prove the fundamental theorem of algebra in the case where $n = 2$.

5. (a) Find a linear order relation in $(C; +, \cdot)$.

(b) If L is a linear order relation in $(C; +, \cdot)$, then either 1L0 or 0L1, but not both. Denote by $\mathcal{P}_L$ the class of all elements of C which bear the same relation to 0 as does 1. That is, if 1L0, then α is in $\mathcal{P}_L$ if and only if αL0; and if 0L1, then α is in $\mathcal{P}_L$ if and only if 0Lα. Call the elements of $\mathcal{P}_L$ *positive* (with respect to L). Consider the propositions

$$\begin{cases} \alpha L\beta \text{ implies } \alpha + \gamma L\beta + \gamma; \\ \alpha L\beta, \gamma \text{ in } \mathcal{P}_L \text{ implies } \alpha\gamma L\beta\gamma. \end{cases} \tag{*}$$

Prove that not both propositions in (*) are true for your linear order relation in part (a);

(c) Prove that *no* linear order relation in $(C; +, \cdot)$ satisfies (*). [*Hint:* Assume (*). Show that if 0Lα, then $-\alpha$L0. Now if 0L1, each of 0Li and iL0 leads to 0L-1, which is impossible. Similar reasoning leads to a contradiction if 1L0.]

APPENDIX C

Peano Postulates

In our development we began with the usual properties of the positive integers. We might well ask if the system of positive integers cannot be built up from more "primitive" notions. It can indeed. We state here a system of five axioms from which the system of positive integers, as we know that system, can be developed. The axioms give five properties which an assumed collection of objects, called natural numbers, is to have.

(1) 1 is a natural number.

(2) For each natural number x there exists exactly one natural number, called the successor of x, which will always be denoted by x'.

(3) We always have $x' \neq 1$.

(4) If $x' = y'$, then $x = y$.

(5) If S is a collection of natural numbers such that

(i) 1 belongs to S,

(ii) if x belongs to S, x' belongs to S,

then S contains all natural numbers.

These axioms (or postulates) are referred to as the *Peano postulates*. As we said, they suffice for the construction of the system $(Z; +, \cdot \,; <)$. We can even ask for a reduction of these to a more primitive level, and this also has been done. However, we do not dwell on this here.

For further information see references 10, 11, 14 (p. 142).

Turning an Error to Good Advantage

If a beginning algebra student (who has not yet studied quadratic equations and knows nothing of square roots) is asked to solve the equation

$$x^2 - 2 = 0,$$

he might reason as follows:

Add 1 to both sides, getting $x^2 - 1 = 1$.
Factor the left side into $(x - 1)(x + 1)$.
Divide the equation $(x - 1)(x + 1) = 1$ by $x + 1$ and obtain the equation

$$x - 1 = \frac{1}{1 + x}.$$

Add 1 to both sides, getting

$$x = 1 + \frac{1}{1 + x}.$$

Of course *we* all know that this solution is no good, since it doesn't really solve the equation for x—we must know x in order to find x from *this* result.

However, our beginning algebra student may show this result to a friend who knows no algebra whatever and tell his friend the objections we have to his solution. The friend may then look at the problem and say "Well, that's easily fixed. We will just get rid of the x on the right by substituting for it what it equals." Thus:

$$x = 1 + \frac{1}{1 + x} = 1 + \cfrac{1}{1 + \left(1 + \cfrac{1}{1 + x}\right)}$$

133

$$= 1 + \cfrac{1}{2 + \cfrac{1}{1 + \left(1 + \cfrac{1}{1 + x}\right)}}$$

$$= 1 + \cfrac{1}{2 + \cfrac{1}{2 + \cfrac{1}{1 + \left(1 + \cfrac{1}{1 + x}\right)}}}$$

. . . .

Thus, the answer is

$$x = 1 + \cfrac{1}{2 + \cfrac{1}{2 + \cfrac{1}{2 + \cfrac{1}{2 + \cdots}}}} \tag{1}$$

What are we going to say to this?

We will not proceed further with this mythical conversation. We *know* that the solutions of $x^2 - 2 = 0$ are $x = \sqrt{2}$ and $x = -\sqrt{2}$. Thus, if the right side of (1) is meaningful at all, it would seem reasonable to say that it was equal to one of $\sqrt{2}, -\sqrt{2}$.

Our problem then is to attempt to attach some meaning to the right side of (1), independent of the process used in deriving it. We might, for example, stop the process at various stages and see what kinds of numbers we get. Thus, we might examine the sequence.

$$1, \; 1 + \frac{1}{2}, \; 1 + \cfrac{1}{2 + \cfrac{1}{2}}, \; 1 + \cfrac{1}{2 + \cfrac{1}{2 + \cfrac{1}{2}}}, \; 1 + \cfrac{1}{2 + \cfrac{1}{2 + \cfrac{1}{2 + \cfrac{1}{2}}}}, \; \cdots.$$

Computing these terms gives

$$1, \frac{3}{2}, \frac{7}{5}, \frac{17}{12}, \frac{41}{29}, \; \cdots.$$

We might expect that if the right side of (1) has any meaning, then the numbers in this sequence are better and better approximations to its value. Thus, these terms might be expected to be closer and closer to the solution of the equation $x^2 - 2 = 0$. Let us designate the terms by $x_1, x_2, x_3, \cdots$. Then

$$x_1 = 1, \, x_2 = \frac{3}{2}, \, x_3 = \frac{7}{5}, \, x_4 = \frac{17}{12}, \, x_5 = \frac{41}{29}, \cdots. \qquad (2)$$

To check our expectations, we examine the differences $x_1^2 - 2$, $x_2^2 - 2, x_3^2 - 2, \cdots$.

$$x_1^2 - 2 = 1^2 - 2 = -1,$$

$$x_2^2 - 2 = \left(\frac{3}{2}\right)^2 - 2 = \frac{9}{4} - 2 = \frac{1}{4} = \frac{1}{2^2},$$

$$x_3^2 - 2 = \left(\frac{7}{5}\right)^2 - 2 = \frac{49}{25} - 2 = -\frac{1}{25} = -\frac{1}{5^2},$$

$$x_4^2 - 2 = \left(\frac{17}{12}\right)^2 - 2 = \frac{189}{144} - 2 = \frac{1}{144} = \frac{1}{12^2}.$$

Indeed, our expectations seem to be borne out. Each x_n^2 is closer to 2 than is the preceding one. Indeed, the data so far leads to the almost inescapable conclusion that if

$$x_n = \frac{h_n}{k_n}$$

(we assume h_n and k_n have no common divisor greater than 1), then

$$x_n^2 - 2 = (-1)^n \cdot \frac{1}{k_n^2}. \qquad (3)$$

At least this equation is true for $n = 1, 2, 3, 4$. Note, however, that even if we knew this last equation, we could not be sure $x_n^2 - 2$ was always getting numerically smaller as n grew larger unless we knew k_n was growing larger with n. Let us try to prove equation (3) and also prove that k_n is increasing without bound as n increases.

We first note that

$$x_3 = 1 + \frac{1}{2 + \dfrac{1}{2}} = 1 + \frac{1}{1 + 1 + \dfrac{1}{2}} = 1 + \frac{1}{1 + x_2},$$

$$x_4 = 1 + \cfrac{1}{2 + \cfrac{1}{2 + \cfrac{1}{2}}} = 1 + \cfrac{1}{1 + 1 + \cfrac{1}{2 + \cfrac{1}{2}}}$$

$$= 1 + \cfrac{1}{1 + x_3},$$

and so on. In the same way

$$x_{n+1} = 1 + \frac{1}{1 + x_n}$$

for all n. Hence, from $x_n = \dfrac{h_n}{k_n}$, $x_{n+1} = \dfrac{h_{n+1}}{k_{n+1}}$ we conclude

$$\frac{h_{n+1}}{k_{n+1}} = 1 + \cfrac{1}{1 + \cfrac{h_n}{k_n}} = 1 + \frac{k_n}{h_n + k_n} = \frac{h_n + 2k_n}{h_n + k_n}.$$

Since h_n and k_n have no common divisor greater than 1, we must have

$$\begin{cases} h_{n+1} = h_n + 2k_n, \\ k_{n+1} = h_n + k_n. \end{cases} \tag{4}$$

The reader might well extend the sequence given in (2) by making use of these equations. Doing so yields the next three terms:

$$x_6 = \frac{99}{70}, x_7 = \frac{239}{169}, x_8 = \frac{577}{408}.$$

(It might be noted that x_8 is already correct to five decimal places as an approximation to $\sqrt{2}$.)

The reader should have no trouble at all in convincing himself [from equations (4)] that k_n does indeed continually increase with increasing n and that there is no number greater than all k_n.

We now return to equation (3), which we know to be true for $n = 1, 2, 3, 4$. Let us suppose (3) is true for all $n \leq q$. Then for $n = q$ in (3) we have

$$x_q^2 - 2 = (-1)^q \cdot \frac{1}{k_q^2}.$$

On the other hand, since $x_q = \dfrac{h_q}{k_q}$, we also have

$$x_q^2 - 2 = \frac{h_q^2}{k_q^2} - 2 = \frac{h_q^2 - 2k_q^2}{k_q^2} \,.$$

From these two expressions for $x_q^2 - 2$ we find

$$(-1)^q \cdot \frac{1}{k_q^2} = \frac{h_q^2 - 2k_q^2}{k_q^2} \,,$$

and therefore,

$$h_q^2 - 2k_q^2 = (-1)^q \,. \qquad\qquad (5)$$

Finally,

$$x_{q+1}^2 - 2 = \frac{h_{q+1}^2}{k_{q+1}^2} - 2 = \frac{h_{q+1}^2 - 2k_{q+1}^2}{k_{q+1}^2}$$

$$= \frac{(h_q + 2k_q)^2 - 2(h_q + k_q)^2}{k_{q+1}^2} \quad \text{(by (4))}^{\cdot}$$

$$= -\,\frac{h_q^2 - 2k_q^2}{k_{q+1}^2}$$

$$= (-1)^{q+1} \cdot \frac{1}{k_{q+1}^2} \quad \text{(by (5))}.$$

Therefore, (3) is also true for $q + 1$ and hence is completely proved by mathematical induction.

Since k_n is increasing and grows arbitrarily large, we can say that $(-1)^n \cdot (1/k_n^2)$, and hence $x_n^2 - 2$, tends to 0 as n increases indefinitely. This means that x_n itself tends to $\sqrt{2}$. Thus, if we interpret the right side of (1) as meaning the limit of the x_n obtained from it by cutting off the tails of the "continuous fraction," we see that not only is the expression meaningful, it is even correct as a root of the equation $x^2 - 2 = 0$. Further, the expression can be used for the computation of $\sqrt{2}$ to any desired degree of accuracy.

● EXERCISES

1. Show that in the above we have solved exercise 8, p. 76.

2. What about the other root, $-\sqrt{2}$, of $x^2 - 2 = 0$?

3. Parallel the entire development above using the equation $x^2 - 5 = 0$. Use your result to compute $\sqrt{5}$ correct to five decimal places.

4. Show that things are not so nice for $x^2 - 3 = 0$.

5. Generalize the text results for equations of the form $x^2 - (s^2 + 1) = 0$, where s is a positive integer.

6. Prove that the h_n, k_n appearing in the text discussion are given by:

$$h_n = \frac{1}{2} \{(1 + \sqrt{2})^n + (1 - \sqrt{2})^n\} \ ,$$

$$k_n = \frac{1}{2\sqrt{2}} \{(1 + \sqrt{2})^n - (1 - \sqrt{2})^n\} \ .$$

[*Hint:* The easiest way is to verify that these are correct for $n = 1$ and then show that these expressions satisfy equations (4).]

The right side of (1) is called a *continued fraction*, and the x_n are called *convergents* to the continued fraction. Every real number can be expressed in terms of such continued fractions. One very interesting feature of the convergents of the continued fraction expansion of an irrational number is the following.

If a/b (a and b being integers) is a convergent to the continued fraction expansion of an irrational number α, then no other rational c/d with $d < b$ is as close to α as is a/b. For instance, in our example with the $\sqrt{2}$ this theorem tells us that if a rational number c/d is as close to $\sqrt{2}$ as is $577/408$, then $d > 408$.

The proof is too long to be included here. We illustrate the theorem by one more example. Suppose we know π to have the value 3.14159 correct to five decimal places. Then we can write

$$\pi = 3 + .14159 \cdots = 3 + \cfrac{1}{\cfrac{1}{.14159 \cdots}}$$

$$= 3 + \cfrac{1}{7 + .0626 \cdots} = 3 + \cfrac{1}{7 + \cfrac{1}{\cfrac{1}{.0626 \cdots}}}$$

$$= 3 + \cfrac{1}{7 + \cfrac{1}{15 + .9 \cdots}} = 3 + \cfrac{1}{7 + \cfrac{1}{15 + \cfrac{1}{\cfrac{1}{.9 \cdots}}}}$$

$$= 3 + \cfrac{1}{7 + \cfrac{1}{15 + \cfrac{1}{1 + \cdots}}}$$

The first four convergents are

$$x_1 = 3,$$

$$x_2 = 3 + \frac{1}{7} = \frac{22}{7},$$

$$x_3 = 3 + \cfrac{1}{7 + \cfrac{1}{15}} = \frac{333}{106},$$

$$x_4 = 3 + \cfrac{1}{7 + \cfrac{1}{15 + \cfrac{1}{1}}} = \frac{355}{113}.$$

This set of four approximations to π contains all those which have been most popular in the past. It should be noted that the first six decimal places in $355/113$ are correct. If another rational number is as close to π as is $355/113$, then it has denominator larger than 113.

Before closing we wish to make one more series of observations concerned with our discussion of $\sqrt{2}$. From (3) we see

$$x_n^2 - 2 = \frac{h_n^2}{k_n^2} - 2 = \frac{h_n^2 - 2k_n^2}{k_n^2} = (-1)^n \frac{1}{k_n^2}.$$

Therefore,

$$h_n^2 - 2k_n^2 = (-1)^n.$$

From this we find, for each integer q,

$$h_{2q}^2 - 2k_{2q}^2 = (-1)^{2q} = 1.$$

Thus, the pair (h_{2q}, k_{2q}) is a solution of the equation

$$x^2 - 2y^2 = 1. \qquad (6)$$

(Such an equation to be solved in integers is called a *Diophantine equation*.)

We found above that the values of (h_{2q}, k_{2q}) for $q = 1, 2, 3, 4$, respectively, are $(3, 2)$, $(17, 12)$, $(99, 70)$, $(577, 408)$. These do give solutions to (5), since

$$3^2 - 2 \cdot 2^2 \quad = 1,$$
$$17^2 - 2 \cdot 12^2 \quad = 1,$$
$$99^2 - 2 \cdot 70^2 \quad = 1,$$
$$577^2 - 2 \cdot 408^2 = 1.$$

From exercise 6, p. 138, we know, for all q, that

$$h_{2q} = \frac{1}{2}\{(1 + \sqrt{2})^{2q} + (1 - \sqrt{2})^{2q}\}$$

$$= \frac{1}{2}\{((1 + \sqrt{2})^2)^q + ((1 - \sqrt{2})^2)^q\}$$

$$= \frac{1}{2}\{(3 + 2\sqrt{2})^q + (3 - 2\sqrt{2})^q\},$$

and similarly,

$$k_{2q} = \frac{1}{2\sqrt{2}}\{(3 + 2\sqrt{2})^q - (3 - 2\sqrt{2})^q\}.$$

Therefore, our conclusions above have shown that for every non-negative integer q we may put

$$x = \frac{1}{2}\{(3 + 2\sqrt{2})^q + (3 - 2\sqrt{2})^q\},$$
$$y = \frac{1}{2\sqrt{2}}\{(3 + 2\sqrt{2})^q - (3 - 2\sqrt{2})^q\} \qquad (7)$$

and have a solution of equation (6).

It is true, but we shall not prove it here that every pair of positive integers x, y which satisfy (6) can be obtained from (7) by suitable choice of q.

As the reader may suspect, our whole discussion is merely a fragment of a far more extensive theory. Indeed, the reader may take our discussion as the starting point for his own development of such a theory. Those who wish to read about such things may consult references 4, 6 or 8. For a discussion along the lines of this appendix we especially recommend reference 6.

References

1. R. Courant and H. Robbins, *What is Mathematics?* Oxford, 1941.
2. G. Birkhoff and S. MacLane, *A Survey of Modern Algebra*, Macmillan, 1953.
3. T. Dantzig, *Number, the Language of Science*, Anchor, 1956.
4. H. Davenport, *The Higher Arithmetic*, Hutchinson, 1952.
5. P. Halmos, *Naive Set Theory*, van Nostrand, 1960.
6. A. O. Gelfond, *The Solution of Equations in Integers*, Freeman, 1961.
7. G. H. Hardy, *A Course of Pure Mathematics*, Cambridge, 1947.
8. G. H. Hardy and E. M. Wright, *Introduction to the Theory of Numbers*, Oxford, 1938.
9. E. Kamke, *Theory of Sets*, Dover, 1950.
10. R. B. Kershner and L. R. Wilcox, *The Anatomy of Mathematics*, Ronald, 1950.
11. E. Landau, *Foundations of Analysis*, Chelsea, 1951.
12. I. Niven, *Irrational Numbers*, Wiley, 1956.
13. D. Pedoe, *The Gentle Art of Mathematics*, Macmillan, 1959.
14. B. Russell, *Introduction to Mathematical Philosophy*, Unwin, 1950.
15. W. W. Sawyer, *A Concrete Approach to Abstract Algebra*, Freeman, 1959.
16. W. Sierpinski, *Cardinal and Ordinal Numbers*, Hafner, 1958.
17. H. S. Thurston, *The Number System*, Interscience, 1956.
18. F. Waismann, *Introduction to Mathematical Thinking*, Harpers, 1959.

Index

Throughout the text and the index the following symbols are used:

Z   the set of natural numbers,
R   the set of positive rational numbers,
R⁺ the set of nonnegative real numbers,
R# the set of real numbers,
C   the set of complex numbers.

A reference such as 64(ex. 5) means exercise 5 on page 64. All other references are to pages.

$$\frac{\overset{15}{2}}{15 - 17}$$

$$\frac{\overset{10}{2}}{12 - 10}$$